Achieving Quality Learning in Higher Education

PEGGY NIGHTINGALE AND MIKE O'NEIL

KOGAN
PAGE

London • Philadelphia

First published in 1994

Kogan Page Limited
120 Pentonville Road
London N1 9JN

British Library Cataloguing in Publication Data

A CIP record for this book is available from the British Library.

ISBN 0 7494 1325 5

Typeset by Saxon Graphics Ltd, Derby.
Printed and bound in Great Britain by Biddles Ltd, Guildford and King's Lynn.

Contents

Notes on Contributors

Authors

Peggy Nightingale is Director of the Professional Development Centre at the University of New South Wales. Her published work comes from her discipline background in English Literature as well as her interests in postgraduate supervision, students' writing, gender, training and development, and quality in higher education. She has recently been granted a commission by the Australian Committee for the Advancement of University Teaching to produce assessing and examining materials for use by Australian universities.

Mike O'Neil is Principal Lecturer in Higher Education at Nottingham Trent University. Over the last 12 years he has worked in the field of educational and staff development in three universities (Teesside, Nottingham Trent and The University of Western Australia) and for the CVCP/Universities' Staff Development Unit in Sheffield. His extensive consultancy, research and development work in universities has been matched by many publications on appraisal and evaluation, quality of teaching, student learning, and staff development policy and practice.

Case study writers

Ronald Barnett is Reader in Higher Education at the Institute of Education, University of London. His books include *The Idea of Higher Education* and *Improving Higher Education: Total Quality Care*.

Priscilla Chadwick is Dean of Educational Development at South Bank University where she coordinates staff development and quality issues in teaching and learning. She is a regular broadcaster for the BBC and has a number of publications and wide experience in the field of education.

Ken Onion is Senior Lecturer in Psychology in the Faculty of Education at Nottingham Trent University where he coordinates the outcomes-based degree course in human and education studies. His chief research interest is in the relationship between teachers' philosophies of pedagogy and their wider belief systems.

Gus Pennington is Head of Educational Development Services at the University of Teesside. He has research and consultancy interests in organizational learning and has published widely in the fields of staff development, appraisal and action inquiry. Since 1992 he has been a quality auditor for the Higher Education Quality Council and has more recently been a part-time advisor for the CVCP/Universities' Staff Development Unit in Sheffield.

Douglas Porter is Secretary and Registrar of the University of Queensland. He has wide responsibilities for coordinating central administrative services and was heavily involved in the preparation of the university's first quality portfolio.

Peter Taylor is now a lecturer in the School of Learning and Development at Queensland University of Technology, after some 18 years of secondary teaching. His areas of teaching and research include social-cognitive perspectives on teaching and learning and the application of those perspectives to the design of more effective contexts for learning.

Ortrun Zuber-Skerritt is a full-time associate professor in higher education at Griffith University (Brisbane) and a part-time faculty member of the International Management Centre (Pacific Region). She is the author of *Action Research in Higher Education* and *Professional Development in Higher Education*, both published by Kogan Page.

Chapter 1

Defining Quality

In London the Centre for Higher Education Studies and the Committee of Directors of Polytechnics sponsor a seminar titled 'Implementing Total Quality Management in Higher Education'. In Canberra, the Higher Education Council publishes the final version of its advice to the Minister in a paper titled, 'The Quality of Higher Education'. In the United States publishers race to bring out the next definitive statement on managing quality in higher education. Quality is the word. And, unlike 'standards' with all its overtones of élitism, it is not a word people seem to find difficult – except when they are asked to define what they mean by it. Most resort in desperation to Pirsig and *Zen and the Art of Motorcycle Maintenance*. Our concern is with the characteristics of quality and the processes that may contribute to it.

However, we accept the point eloquently developed by our colleague Ron Barnett (1992a) in his recent book *Improving Higher Education* that there is little to be gained in a discussion of quality if you have not clarified what you mean by the term. So let us do a quick run-through of the various versions and declare our position.

The Quality in Higher Education (QHE) Project, based in Birmingham, attempted to develop a methodology for assessing quality in higher education (Harvey *et al.*, 1992). A first step is to clarify the criteria by which different 'stakeholders' would make their judgements. In their summary document, the project team's marketplace orientation to quality emerges:

> There are a number of ways of viewing quality. Traditionally, quality has been linked to the idea of exceptionally high standards. A second approach to quality sees it in terms of consistency. ... Quality in this sense is summed up by the interrelated ideas of *zero defects* and *getting things right the first time*. A third approach to quality relates it to fitness for purpose. ... quality is judged in terms of the extent to which a product or service meets its stated purpose. A fourth approach to quality equates it with value for money. ... A fifth view of quality sees quality as transformative. Education is not a service *for* a customer but an ongoing process of transformation *of* the participant. This leads to two notions of transformative quality in education, enhancing the consumer and empowering the customer. (p.1)

The problem with this approach to quality is not the market orientation. It is the number of assumptions, judgements and ideologies hidden in these five apparently straightforward ways of viewing quality. Barnett (1992a) has unpacked these ideas at some length; drawing on his argument, we would like to explore some of the issues that are buried in this paragraph.

Quality equals high standards. Standards are a set of criteria against which an enterprise is judged, says Barnett (p.55). Whose standards? The QHE project has revealed some common ground in broad terms, but substantial differences arise (Harvey *et al.*, 1992, p.3) between students, staff, managers in higher education, employers, government, validating bodies, assessment bodies and funding councils. But even more important, what can be meaningfully done with those standards? The common position of governments is that universities will have to be judged against their own identified mission and goals because diversity in the system is desirable. As Barnett points out (p.55), if one institution sets itself a task of achieving at a very high level and another is satisfied to perform at a different level, and both are judged to perform equally well in one aspect of their mission – say, teaching – the second might be said to be outperforming the first because it had exceeded its own goals. On another tack, let us take the question of standards of degrees when there is increasing diversity in the system. The notion of 'value-added' has been suggested as a way of levelling the playing field when participants have started from very different positions on the education ladder. So it seems very likely that degrees could be awarded in future to students to whom they would have been denied in the past, and that students who succeed at one university may not have reached a standard acceptable at another where the input standard was higher. Barnett's point is that there can still be a bottom line, one that is dependent on the conception of higher education as, at the very least, fostering higher order intellectual capacities in students:

> unless they were able to form and substantiate independent thought and action in a coherent and articulate fashion, we would have to say that we were not in the presence of 'higher education'. (p.58)

We think this statement could help define a standard for higher education but, in the end, the concept of quality as standards proves to be unproductive in the sense that it says and does nothing about improvement. No matter how comprehensively an institution meets the set standards, it should be thinking about and working toward improvement.

Quality as consistency or zero defects. In that this orientation to quality emphasizes the process, it seems more likely to assist in conceiving what quality might be in higher education. Let's say that we have agreed that getting things right means fostering those higher order intellectual capacities. We can look at the outcomes to reach some conclusions about the quality of an institution. What evidence do students present that they can actually think and act independently, coherently and articulately? There is one problem. As Barnett points out (Chapter 2), the aims of higher education are not achieved by the teachers or administrators. The aims of higher education are achieved by the students. At least in theory it would be possible to get the processes right, offer a programme of study with zero defects and for reasons purely outside the control of the institution – say, a crushing economic disaster affecting all students in the programme – none of them achieves the overarching aim of higher education. Can the institution be judged as of poor quality? The way out of this morass is to decide to judge the processes themselves. To what extent does the institution, or more accurately, its programmes of study, offer intellectual challenges to the students which are likely to result in autonomous, critical, reflective and articulate students? So if we disregard the manufacturing vocabulary of zero defects, and if we can agree about a characteristic that distinguishes and identifies all higher education, plus others perhaps which distinguish particular institutions and courses in a diverse system, and if we do not judge the process by the outcome, this second view of quality might be a bit more helpful than the first. But that asks for a great deal to be discarded and/or agreed.

Quality as fitness for purpose. Barnett argues that fitness for purpose 'can be an ideological term, wearing an apparent democratic concern on its sleeve, but all the while acting as a mask for a *hierarchical* view of higher education' (p.48). So institutions are encouraged to find their own niche in the system, but in this diversity, some purposes attract more esteem than others and, hence, are judged to be of higher quality (and may be resourced in accordance with that judgement). All institutions are equal, but some are more equal than others. The other interpretation of fitness for purpose is of a *parallel* approach to quality assessment – institutions are equal but different, and no comparisons may be drawn. Carried to its extreme, this would mean that anything goes. A university may describe itself in any terms at all, set any mission, be fit for any purpose. It is not just that we keep stumbling over questions of whose purposes when we talk about fitness for purpose, it is that there is a basic logical incoherence in the approaches to quality that this view requires. But if we could agree on a unifying purpose, perhaps quality judgements could be made.

Quality as value for money. Once again we have to ask what is valuable to whom. The arguments are like those applying to standards and fitness for purpose. In addition, this view of quality forces us into input-output measures when what we really should be looking at are the processes if we seek improvement. If our conception of higher education is that it develops higher order intellectual capacities, and that this is its essence, the one purpose which is identical in all institutions and without which they cannot claim to be institutions of higher education, we cannot let quality be judged on grounds such as how many students can be pushed through the system at how low a unit cost. Barnett characterizes this as the black box view of higher education: 'it does not matter what goes on in the black box as long as the quantity of desired inputs and outputs is achieved' (p.20).

The demand for more and more evaluation and the application of performance indicators is an example of this black box approach. Many assumptions lie behind the notion that if there are data revealing some deviation from the norm, knowing the deviation will cause change for the better. Some of those assumptions may be valid – at least in a way – but others are dangerous. We are not going to have high quality learning just because there is a favourable staff/student ratio and a low rate of attrition in a department of a university, or any other combination of simplistic input-output measures. Perhaps the biggest danger is diverting attention and resources from the important and complex question of how can we achieve the conditions in which high quality learning is likely to take place to much less important questions of how can we collect the masses of data required for purposes of accountability. The universities already provide a great deal of information to government statisticians. The important question is whether the institutions or the government make effective use of what they already know. It was a wise person who said, 'Weighing the pig doesn't make it fat'. The corollary is 'If you interrupt its feeding to take it to the scale, it is going to get thin'.

Quality as transformative. Now here we seem to have something because Barnett's and our notion of what is the essence of higher education is exactly this, transforming the student, empowering her and enhancing her by developing higher order intellectual capacities which allow her to critique her experience and herself. We have a few problems with the shift in the language in the QHE report from 'participant' to 'consumer'. The paradigm shift involved in accepting the notion that achievement of the goals of higher education is in the hands of the students requires something much more like participant than consumer. Also the view of quality in higher education as transformative requires a vision of the teacher as facilitator (Biggs, 1989) not as salesperson, and the student as active and committed participant.

What we have done so far is contrast two notions of quality – perhaps a bit unfairly because we have opposed one paragraph from a summary document with a fully developed philosophical and sociological argument. We have said that our concern is with the characteristics of quality and the processes that contribute to it. It is important for us to lay our cards on the table and say we agree with Ron Barnett. The essence of higher education lies in the intellectual challenge presented to students. Some institutions will also be concerned with basic research; some with applied research. Some institutions will emphasize their service role within their community; some will emphasize the education of traditional residential undergraduates. Some will contribute professional education and/or vocationally oriented courses; others will stress a liberal or general education. Regardless of the many variations possible within the diverse systems of higher education developing throughout the world, there is one overarching purpose that all share – fostering higher order intellectual capabilities in their students no matter who they are and at what stage of their studies. That is what we must all be concerned with in the long run. We will characterize high quality learning later, but our view is in tune with Barnett's – we simply elaborate it in different terms.

Thus, we wish to move away from what we believe to be increasingly pointless arguments about whether students are inputs or outputs, or what the product of higher education might be. We could not agree with Ellis (1993b) that teaching materials or teachers' behaviours are the products of higher education to which BS5750 standards ought to be applied, but to argue at length about the teacher-centred, student-as-irresponsible-sponge images of education this notion suggests to us would be diverting attention from the real issue which we believe is whether graduates are 'able to form and substantiate independent thought and action in a coherent and articulate fashion'. If someone finds that referring to students as inputs or as customers and teaching materials as products helps them plan a strategy which leads to high quality learning which they can demonstrate by reviewing outcomes, well, we might not find the approach congenial, but if it works for them, fine. For us, thinking of our students as participants in the learning process or as partners who share their learning with us or as members of the university community helps us maintain focus on creating the conditions we believe necessary to foster high quality learning, but we aren't going to argue about it. We prefer to expend energy on concern about demands from others for quality assurance requirements which undermine the possibility that high quality learning will be achieved. For instance, as Elton (1993, p.141) points out in his discussion of English and Scottish Funding Council quality audits, 'This direct coupling of quality assessment to funding decisions has serious dangers, in that it removes any real ownership of the assessment from the HEIs [higher education institutions]'.

This book will be about quality in higher education, in particular quality of teaching and learning, and about enhancing quality. Quality is already present in higher education in all of the systems with which the authors of this book are familiar. That is not, however, to say that those systems cannot be improved. Indeed, demands for improvement have been coming thick and fast for the past decade; unfortunately, those demands are rarely accompanied by acknowledgement of the existing quality and as one might expect, they are greeted with defensiveness and counter-attack. Just as we do not want to buy into attempts to define quality in higher education past that overarching conception of the ultimate mission of all higher education, neither do we want to become entrapped in charge and counter-charge about whose fault it might be that perfection has not yet been achieved.

Our concern is to try to discover how the various elements which interact to produce higher education as we currently know it may be encouraged to interact to produce higher education as we would like it to be, meeting the challenges of a changing world without sacrificing the achievements of the past. For many reasons, the interaction of a host of agents seems increasingly important in any discussion of higher education and quality. Those interactions will figure largely in this volume.

The approach of this book

To give an overview of this book: we begin by summarizing some of the statements, policies and recommendations of stakeholders (governments, employers, students, universities and their staff) in higher education on the question of quality and comment generally on some of the assumptions about teaching and learning and higher education that are revealed in those materials. Next, we try to step back from the detail which seems to dominate discussions of quality and ask, what are the characteristics of high quality learning and what are the conditions which are necessary to foster it?

We proceed to argue that if high quality learning is to be encouraged, all stakeholders in higher education need to understand learning better than they apparently do at this time. If learning about learning is necessary and we have a pretty good idea about how to encourage high quality learning, what is the logical design of a programme of quality improvement which will simultaneously foster high quality learning about learning by all concerned so that a continuous process of improvement begins? We look at action research and total quality management as strategies and suggest that either or both can provide a model in which both individual and organizational learning may occur. Finally, we return to the question of accountability and quality assurance and suggest that once again, trying to focus on the important issue of encouraging high quality learning may help to reduce wasted effort and direct energy where it will be usefully expended.

We offer a framework for reconsidering what has become a tortuous and convoluted argument among the various stakeholders about the nature of quality, how to measure it and how to promote it, and we offer a strategy for promoting continuous improvement and judging whether the main purpose of all institutions of higher education is being achieved. We offer a strategy but not tactics, which must be determined within the context of specific institutions and systems. The strategy involves promoting change and addressing the causes of resistance to change, but we do not suggest who the change agent(s) should be. We expect that staff developers will be involved but they may not be the driving force; too often simplistic assumptions are made that with some good will, some coercion and a lot of staff development, major change will take place. Just as the responsibility for high quality learning cannot be borne by academic staff alone, neither can the responsibility for promoting change be passed on to staff developers alone. There is a very large community of people involved in, concerned for, and mutually responsible for the quality of higher education; it is time they started acting like a community in the interests of quality.

In addition, we offer case studies of attempts, most of them continuing, to promote quality in institutions of higher education. These case studies are incorporated into the chapters where they are most relevant to the argument as it develops. Tactics, and assessments of their efficacy, are in these cases. We have collected material from institutions in Australia and the United Kingdom and have sought to present different approaches. As always we have learned from writing; we have also learned from our collaborators on this project and we are grateful to them for their contributions.

We have written informally and often in the first person in the hope that readers will join in the dialogue and learn with us. Preparing this book has convinced us that the learning must be as continuous as the improvement.

Chapter 2

Demands for Quality Assurance

Late in 1993 Australian universities were visited for one day by small sub-committees (four people) representing the Committee for Quality Assurance in Higher Education (CQAHE) which was given the task of recommending to the Minister of Employment, Education and Training how A$75 million of 'reward money' for quality should be distributed among the nearly 40 universities in Australia. It was known that the Committee was required to discover rewardable quality in no more than 50 per cent of the institutions. The reasoning was that institutions do not deserve a reward for simply 'doing their job'; that is what they are funded to do. This money was to be an incentive to excel.

Each institution had been 'invited' to prepare and submit a document no more than 20 pages long making its case for claiming some of this reward; institutions did not have to participate but with some A$10 million at stake for some of them, it was unlikely they would not join the game. The institutions could supplement the short document with appendices incorporating data to demonstrate their effectiveness. They were given only a few weeks and very little concrete direction about what to submit, except that they were to cover teaching, research and community service; the CQAHE did not even discuss what criteria would be applied until after the portfolios were submitted.

To some extent the universities were shooting in the dark in trying to provide winning answers to the Committee's questions:

- What quality assurance policies and practices does the institution have in place or is it developing?
- How effective are these?
- How does the institution judge the quality of its outcomes?
- In what areas and in what ways are the outcomes excellent?
- What are the institution's priorities for improvement?

However, some clues were provided to those who had followed the debates and poured over the documents of the previous five years. Unfortunately, the clues were often ambiguous, even contradictory and, as we shall see, some could possibly encourage institutions to take actions which might undermine efforts to encourage high quality student learning.

Colleagues in institutions in the United Kingdom had been receiving similar visits from Audit and Assessment teams established respectively by the Higher Education Quality Council and the various Higher Education Funding Councils.

Decoding government demands for quality assurance

In both the United Kingdom and Australia national governments have expended a great deal of effort to bring about massive change to the systems of higher education; the principle documents outlining these changes are two UK White Papers (DES, 1987, 1991), an Australian White Paper (Dawkins, 1988) and several Australian Higher Education Council documents (HEC, 1990, 1992a, 1992c). Oddly enough, much that has happened under a Conservative government in Britain and under a Labour government in Australia has resulted in similar outcomes: the abolition of binary systems, forced amalgamations of smaller institutions, overhaul of the various government bodies advising on and regulating higher education, changed funding bases, reduction of resources, increased numbers of students, improved access for 'non-traditional' students and so on.

1987 United Kingdom: Higher Education: Meeting the Challenge

The 1987 UK White Paper expressed an important aim of expanding higher education provision at the least cost to the national purse. It also established a dual funding system for institutions on each side of the binary line: the Universities' Funding Council (UFC) and the Polytechnics' and Colleges' Funding Council (PCFC). One result was that the PCFC introduced competition into its funding methodology by calling on the polytechnic and college sector to bid for some of their student numbers at differential (lower) prices. Quality, alongside price, also figured in this competitive process in that 'high quality' course ratings (as determined by the Council for National Academic Awards and Her Majesty's Inspectorate) resulted in extra cash flowing into the coffers of institutions with 'kitemarked' high quality courses.

The Robbins' Committee's (1963) aims of higher education as 'instruction in skills, advancement of learning, and the transmission of a common culture and common standards of citizenship' were reaffirmed in the 1987 White Paper, alongside a commitment to research and scholarship. But, ominously, an instrumental purpose was added: 'to take increasing account of the economic requirements of the country' (p.2). A clear message to stress 'enterprise' education (anticipating the Enterprise in Higher Education Initiative) and to ensure a closer communion between academics and business people was also conveyed in this Paper. Indeed, this latter connection was heralded as a means 'to more suitable teaching', though the meaning of this entreaty is somewhat mysterious, save for its possible extension to vocational preparation.

A whole chapter in *Meeting the Challenge* (DES, 1987) is devoted to the matter of 'quality and efficiency'. The first sentence in Chapter 3 is noteworthy: 'Higher education is expensive' (p.14). A possible extension with the clause 'and we mean to do something about it' is embedded in this whole document, where an explicit intention to squeeze the HE system even harder in pursuit of yet more efficiency gains is declared.

Quality, claims the UK government, 'depends upon the commitment of the academic community to the maintenance and improvement of standards' (p. 16). In this matter the government plans to establish systems for monitoring the commitment and the outcomes, anticipating the audit and assessment agencies which were to follow the 1991 White Paper.

Quality, too, will be judged, intones the 1987 Paper (pp. 16–18), by three means:

1. 'academic standards of courses' ('fitness for purpose') – what they demand of students, and the extent they meet employers' needs;
2. 'teaching quality' – staff training and development, appraisal systems, evaluation of the results of teaching (note the omission of 'learning'), reports from external examiners and patterns of employment of graduates, involvement of professional practitioners in vocational courses and feedback from students themselves;
3. 'student achievements' – performance indicators to be used include numbers and class of degrees obtained, non-completion rates, acquisition of specialist knowledge and communication/numeracy skills, enterprise, and value-added comparisons, eg, entry qualifications compared with achievements.

1988 Australia: Higher Education: a Policy Statement

In the 1988 Australian White Paper (Dawkins, 1988), the emphasis was also on growth because growth in higher education was considered necessary for the improvement of the nation's economic condition. In other words, higher education has a predominantly instrumental function. Significantly, the reform of higher education took place in a context which linked education with employment and training in a new Ministry of Employment, Education and Training. Frequently the paper linked education and skill development, as when it referred to 'the need for a better educated and more highly skilled population' (p. 4).

The growth was to take place in line with national priorities, as defined by the government. In the introductory pages of the White Paper, unexceptionable goals for the nation were outlined:

- to be a 'fair and free society', hence, improved access to higher education and equity in the distribution of the new places;
- to be a 'rich society intellectually, culturally and economically' and one 'that aspires to excellence and that continually extends its skills and knowledge', hence, the importance of a strong higher education system.

These goals cannot be achieved without a strong economic base, argued the government, so limited resources must be allocated according to national priorities which are 'the fields of engineering, science and technology, and business and management studies' (p.17). Even equity goals are justified in terms of the need for 'a more dynamic and effective skilled workforce' (p.53).

Surprisingly little was said in this Paper about quality; the implicit assumption in the instrumentalist view of higher education is that quality is a matter of fitness for purpose and the government is going to determine what purposes should be emphasized. The first page of the White Paper contains the statement that 'The Government is committed to growth and quality enhancement across the whole of the education and training system...' but the recurring word in the Paper is 'accountability'. The principal mechanism for monitoring the institutions was to be the negotiation of an educational profile which defined the role of the institution, its mission and responsibilities, and which would be used to determine its funding needs and against which the institution's performance would be judged:

> The provision of funds under the agreement will carry with it an obligation by the institution to give due regard to national priorities and to the objectives of improved efficiency and effectiveness. For the institution, the profile will provide a mechanism that balances institutional autonomy and the need for accountability. (p.30)

A brief digression on the Enterprise in Higher Education (EHE) Initiative in the United Kingdom (see Macnair, 1990; Wright, 1992) is warranted at this stage. This initiative was prompted by a similar desire to make higher education more responsive to the needs of the economy. It did not change fundamental values and the ethos of higher education but rather it made more visible and explicit the congruence between the desires of employers (eg, increased personal and social skills for graduates) and the goals of educators who sought to foster a 'deep' approach to learning. Where these initiatives took root, the learning climate shifted from being dominated by a transmission-of-information model to one which attempted to facilitate meaningful learning and develop transferable skills. Tate (1993, p.290) lists the 16 competences adopted by the University of Ulster's EHE programme, including 'problem analysis and solving – logical thought, ability to identify key issues and create solutions' and, as she says,

> These competencies are not simply technical or instrumental, or knee jerk reactions to the demands of industry. ... they present a worthwhile undertaking in relation to the values of higher education regardless of their utility for the immediate demands of industry. (p.291)

There has been no parallel initiative in Australia.

Vague references were made throughout the Australian White Paper to the intention to grant resources on the basis of performance:

> The Government supports the development of a funding system that responds to institutional performance and the achievement of mutually agreed goals. It intends to develop funding arrangements that take into account a range of output, quality and performance measures.... (Dawkins, 1988, p.85)

At this stage it seemed clear that the government had every intention of using performance indicators such as those employed in the United Kingdom to decide on distribution of resources among the various competing institutions.

1991 United Kingdom: Higher Education: A New Framework

Overall, this White Paper (DES, 1991) abolished the binary line, established Funding Councils for England, Wales and Scotland each with its own quality assessment unit, and established (under the control of all UK universities through the Higher Education Quality Council) a UK-wide quality audit unit. An ominous feature of this Paper is the expectation that the Funding Councils would explore ways of informing potential students and employers 'about the actual and relative quality of institutions and of the courses they provide' (p.30).

In terms of teaching, Chapter 2 of the White Paper makes a number of suggestions, some of which are carried over from the 1987 White Paper:

- elements of institutional funding to be linked to assessment (para. 21);
- quality will be taken into account on a common basis in the funding of all higher education institutions (para. 24);
- diversity of institutions to be maintained – funding for teaching needs 'to be related to and safeguard the best of the distinctive missions of individual institutions' (p.14); and
- 'vocational studies and widening access (to be) maintained and extended' (para. 24).

In Chapter 3 of the White Paper, dealing with research, there is a statement worthy of close inspection:

> a new structure for public funding of research in higher education ... [means] ... promoting ... effective use of resources ... [so that] ... institutions should be able to compete for research funds; ... research funds should be distributed on the basis of assessment of research quality. (para. 40)

We think that this paragraph dealing with research funding reflects and implies the government's thinking about the future funding of teaching (note: for *research* in this quote read *teaching*).

Consequently, we are left in no doubt that market forces (competition between institutions for students; 'survival of the fittest'), greater efficiency gains ('more for less'), and invidious comparative inspections (leading to league tables of performance) are the motive forces that underlie the UK government's approach to quality.

1990 and 1992 Australia: Higher Education Council Advice to the Minister

By the end of 1990 the structural changes to higher education in Australia, as decreed by the Dawkins White Paper of 1988, were well-established (with the exception of a few amalgamations which were proving problematic and which have, finally, failed). The Higher Education Council, one of the four constituent councils of the National Board of Employment, Education and Training, in its role as independent adviser to the Minister on higher education, offered a paper, *Higher Education: The Challenges Ahead* (HEC, 1990), in which it explored the issues it saw as most pressing and made recommendations to the Minister on these matters.

Higher Education: The Challenges Ahead. The main theme of the paper (HEC, 1990) was that there is, and ought to be, increasing diversity of the student population in higher education and that this diversity, in turn, requires greater diversity of courses and procedures. The major challenge was to provide 'relevant higher education of undisputed quality to a growing and increasingly diverse student body' (p.5).

The HEC advice was that the government should move from targeting school leavers for entry into the extra places being funded in universities and encourage a mix of participants – advice which has been discarded in 1994 with continuing high levels of youth unemployment. The argument originally was that changes in the workplace would increasingly require continuing education of employees throughout their working lives; some of this education and training should happen at the level of higher education.

In this discussion, quality issues were linked to access and diversity and the substantial changes occurring as a result. Recommendations concentrated on rewarding high quality performance in areas other than research and on encouraging good practice in both teaching and university management. 'Quality control' through both internal practices and consultation with external parties was advocated. In particular, greater consultation with employers and professional bodies in the design and evaluation of courses was recommended.

The Council believed that quality need not be adversely affected by broadening the student population mix in higher education, but did recognize that the performance of participants and standards of courses would need to be monitored carefully. There was still a hope that high quality performance could be included in decisions about resource allocation, but the quest for acceptable and useful performance indicators continued. In this discussion, the implicit notion of quality continues to have something to do with fitness for purpose but issues of standards were also being raised, and with considerations of resource allocation a suggestion that quality equals value for money also creeps in.

The emphasis in the White Paper was on directing resources to areas of high national priority and the passing references to the importance of other fields – the humanities in particular – were unconvincing. The tenor of the HEC paper was somewhat different, seeming to try to play down instrumentalism and raise a view of higher education as transformative once again. The Council took a strong stand against courses becoming too specialized and vocationally-oriented. The alternative the HEC suggested was broad, general pre-employment courses followed by specialized on-the-job training and retraining as necessary throughout employment. In addition, higher education was encouraged to develop alternative types of courses such as those which may be studied in modules for specific purposes without making commitments to whole degree programmes. This echoed the switch in the UK towards modular and semesterized undergraduate programmes and the concomitant development of credit accumulation and transfer systems (CATS).

Also in the report were many explicit statements about the importance of adequate resourcing to the maintenance of quality in the system. The HEC seemed less convinced that there was slack left in higher education or that there is an alternative pot of gold. Thus there is at least an implicit acknowledgement that the universities do not carry sole responsibility for the quality of higher education.

Achieving Quality. This document (HEC, 1992c) is the final one in a series (HEC, 1992a, 1992b) to the Minister for Higher Education and Employment Services (then Peter Baldwin) from the Higher Education Council.

The Council emphasizes the very large changes to the higher education system, not just as a result of the White Paper reforms, but also over a 40-year period, and asserts that the concern for quality assurance is primarily prompted by those changes and the importance of knowing their effect. There is also evident a degree of frustration that the universities have failed to respond constructively to repeated calls for public accountability over many years.

The Council starts with a commercial definition of quality which relies on the customers' expectations and perceptions of the product or service. The argument does not take up explicitly the obvious problems with this definition for higher education – the number of 'customers' with different expectations, that some of them are educational novices who cannot know what they ought to expect, that there is no one product or service in higher education and so on. However, the Council finally arrives at 'fitness for purpose'. The Council accepts the position 'that the starting point must be an explication of what is trying to be achieved by a system, institution, or course, and why' (p.6). This is consistent with good practice in curriculum development, assessment and evaluation so should not be contentious as long as the Council does not try to establish unacceptable goals. On the other hand, it also opens the system to the logical fallacy that as long as stated goals are achieved, anything goes.

In fact the Council acknowledges the broad charter of higher education to preserve, share and advance knowledge but it also asserts that these broad goals can only be understood and made operational in a context. Thus, Council says, a national system must have a 'broad, yet definite, statement of purpose' (p.11) which is neither composed of platitudes nor restrictive of institutions' ability to define their own specific missions. It offers the following:

The principal purposes of Australian universities are:

- the education of appropriately qualified Australians to enable them to take a leadership role in the intellectual, cultural, economic and social development of the nation and all its regions;
- the creation and advancement of knowledge; and
- the application of knowledge and discoveries to the betterment of communities in Australia and overseas.

Essentially these purposes recognize that the universities are concerned with teaching, research and community service although, as our review has shown, most of the discussion of quality assurance had been focused on teaching. Indeed there is not much difference between the aims of universities in Australia and in Britain as espoused by governments except for emphasis on, say, 'leadership', and the altruistic value Australians put on overseas aid.

One other issue needs to be highlighted – whose responsibility is quality in higher education? Minister Baldwin's (1991) policy statement which triggered the Council activities on quality stated 'institutions have the major responsibility for ensuring that the teaching process, their research efforts and their graduates are of high quality'. The Council and the institutions have continuously reminded the government that without adequate resources that responsibility cannot be fulfilled. In addition, there are others with responsibilities for making the system of the highest possible quality and constantly improving it. In passing, as it asserts the rights of the various stakeholders, the Council acknowledges that they have obligations as well but very little is made of these obligations.

The second chapter of the paper deals with the Minister's reference: 'the characteristics of quality and its diversity'. The emphasis is on being clear about the objectives of higher education and, in this case, the objectives as related to the attributes of graduates. The view is that there must be more emphasis on developing generic skills and higher order outcomes and less on content; this will be manifest in course and curriculum development, teaching methods and assessment. The question of how the attainment of these higher order skills is to be measured is not adequately dealt with. This issue is supposed to be taken up in the third chapter but all that turns up there is the condemnation of the increasing use of objective tests as promoting and measuring simple recall and a note that academics report the need to rely on such assessment when student: staff ratios are becoming less conducive to interaction and meaningful feedback.

The third chapter deals with factors affecting the quality of higher education. The increased diversity of student populations is not believed necessarily and inevitably to lead to lowered standards. On the quality of teaching the Council accepts the framework for discussion provided by the British PCFC (Warnock, 1990) – five 'necessary conditions...without which good teaching could not exist':

- clarity of aims and objectives;
- a curriculum organization and delivery policy which includes effective methods of promoting learning;
- a policy for the professional development of teaching staff including appointment, induction, appraisal and development;
- means of involving student and employer views in judging the curriculum, its delivery and outcomes; and
- a framework for institutional self-evaluation.

Particular points emphasized in the HEC elaboration are:

- the importance of clear and appropriate aims and objectives;
- the undesirability of over-teaching (too many contact hours) and objective assessment;

- the need for professional development programmes addressing teaching and learning theory at tertiary level;
- support for the use of student assessment of teaching and employer consultation on educational goals and outcomes;
- support for (limited) research in all universities;
- recognition of at least shared responsibility for learning infrastructure between institutions and Commonwealth; and
- recognition of the importance of work of administrators and academic leaders.

At the very least we must acknowledge that this discussion of conditions likely to foster good teaching does not undermine attempts to facilitate transformational learning. Importantly, it acknowledges that there is interaction between elements of the system.

The fourth chapter deals with resource issues. There is acknowledgement of the decline in unit of resource and of the proportion of GDP devoted to higher education. There are also assertions that it is not possible to be certain what impact on quality that decline has had despite many submissions from institutions with qualitative evidence that teaching methods have had to be changed to those less likely to foster higher order learning. The HEC acknowledges that the universities have made substantial efficiency gains (mirroring the same observation made in the 1991 UK White Paper) but suggests that more may be possible if institutions rationalize programmes with very small enrolments. Finally, there is recognition that there are large gaps in funding for libraries, equipment and physical plant.

The concluding chapter takes up the reference asking for strategies to enhance quality and to monitor and evaluate changes in quality over time. The final advice relates to 'possible frameworks and structures that can support a comprehensive approach to quality assurance in Australia's universities' (p.67). The Council reminds us that 'quality assurance' is defined as 'a guarantee that required standards are being met' (p.68) so it seems clear that there will be judgements about the quality of the outcomes as well as the quality of the processes which lead to outcomes. This is an important distinction in that judging quality of outcomes involves evaluation of the goals of an institution – is it doing the right thing? – before judging whether it achieves those goals, while judging the processes involves evaluation of the way an institution sets its goals – for instance, does it consult all stakeholders? – but not of the goals themselves. Thus the Council says,

> Given the diversity of the system and the absence of an acceptable, single, definition of quality, it is up to each institution to define quality in its own way – to set objectives for their programs according to their independent missions and the nature of the outcomes they seek *that are compatible with the purpose and goals of the national system*. (p.67) (our emphasis)

So to this point we have the Council stating that frameworks and structures are needed to guarantee that *required* standards are met and that institutions may define quality for themselves but there should be compatibility with national purposes and goals. A noticeable omission is the suggestion that there will be regular reviews of national goals in consultation with stakeholders who would include leaders of the academic community, though the universities are exhorted to consult and review continuously. In addition we must question a notion of autonomy which says, 'Take any route you want, but go where we tell you'. It is very difficult to see how diversity is to be encouraged under these circumstances.

The advice to the Minister is that universities should be allowed to set their own agendas in another area. The Council calls on universities to develop their own procedures to evaluate the effectiveness of their internal processes for achieving quality; '...the assessment of the quality of the system can then be inferred from the effectiveness of its processes' (p.51). That is, the Council seems to believe that effective means will achieve desirable ends. Finally, the institutions are to be required to hold up for public scrutiny these processes and the evaluation of them. Again we question whether theory in practice will match the espoused theory. Will the Council or the government be satisfied with inference? It seems not, for this introductory passage concludes with a quotation and statements which make very clear that it is not only the processes which should be revealed and evaluated but also that data – hard and soft – are required to prove that there is quality in the institution.

The Minister had foreshadowed his intention to set up some sort of national quality assurance body in his *Quality and Diversity* (Baldwin, 1991) statement. The Council surveys current mechanisms in existence at institutional system level and concludes that although there are many examples of good practice existing mechanisms are not adequate for purposes of accountability.

This completes the story of how the Committee for Quality Assurance in Higher Education (CQAHE) came to be, and of the Australian government's attempts to find a clear stance on which conception of quality would prevail. It seems that in the end (or rather at the time of writing), it is 'fitness for purpose', but there is still a struggle to define purpose and to work out what criteria will apply to the evaluation of fitness. The outcomes, the attributes of graduates as defined so far, are too general and too confused to apply to specific courses and they do not apply as criteria to judge research or community service. Australians were, however, counting their blessings that they were not submitting to both academic audit and assessment of teaching and of research under the auspices of three different bodies, as were their colleagues in the United Kingdom. Nor was base funding linked to assessment in Australia; the Australian 'quality money' was a reward on top of base funding.

We would argue that if the governments were to achieve their goal of improving higher education, institutions would be pressured into quality enhancement programmes which have wide and substantial impact on staff at all levels within the university. The case study which follows reveals what happened in one Australian university prior to the CQAHE visit.

CASE STUDY

An institution responds to the Committee for Quality Assurance in Higher Education

Douglas Porter, University of Queensland

The Higher Education Council (1992c) advice to the Minister defined 'quality' in the following terms:

> The Council sees the focus on outcome, the fitness for purpose, as fundamental to understanding how each of the processes within institutions are organised and evaluated in order to ensure the quality of outcome.

The Council went on to define three broad principles as the basis for its work:

- the attributes acquired by graduates provide the ultimate test of the quality of the system;
- the judgement about the value of the individual processes that combine to lead to quality outcomes rests with the universities, their faculties or schools and their departments – the internal stakeholders, and to an extent, with the peers; and
- the major criterion to be applied to the judgement of the quality of the individual elements of learning programmes should be linked to the contribution that it makes to the staged development of students.

The HEC definition and associated principles open up the possibility of defining *purpose* in terms of institutional mission and goals and *quality* as how successful each university is in pursuing that mission and achieving its goals. Superficially attractive as such a definition is it does, however, raise a number of fundamental questions. Whose purpose? How is purpose defined? Is anyone going to make a judgement about the appropriateness of the mission and goals?

These questions, to some extent, were addressed in research commissioned by the Department of Employment, Education and Training to identify a conceptual framework for considering quality management and quality audit in Australian Universities. This research (Warren Piper, 1993), among other things, provided a framework to assist a university to describe its existing quality assurance procedures and mechanisms.

The appendix to this report included information supplied by eight universities to illustrate the range and types of approaches to quality assurance currently undertaken by institutions. The information provided by the University of Queensland showed that the university already had in place an extensive range of quality assurance procedures within the suggested conceptual framework which covered the following eight provinces of activity:

- educational programmes
- research
- community service
- staff
- students
- academic support services
- resources and assets
- the general governance of the university.

Identifying the various procedures under these headings was not a difficult task, required little consultation and indeed was largely achieved one evening by the author and a colleague over a St Lucia pavement café dinner table. The university's main method of quality assurance in its teaching and learning areas – for example, a systematic review of academic departments on a ten-year cycle – had been in place for almost ten years. What clearly emerged, however, was the rather unstructured and *ad hoc* manner in which the university, over time, had addressed issues of quality assurance.

When the issue was considered by the university's major planning committee – the University Resource and Planning Committee – in the light of the information contained in the appendix to *Quality Management in Universities* (Warren Piper, 1993), it was quickly agreed that the information provided a sound basis for the development of a quality management and assurance plan which would be added to the university's educational profile as a separate and distinctive component.

An institutional quality management and assurance plan

The University Resource and Planning Committee established a small working party led by the president of the academic board to develop the plan. After consultation with senior academic managers, including heads of departments and deans of faculties, this working party recommended that the university's approach to quality assurance should be based on the following principles and strategies:

- quality assurance procedures should promote the achievement of the goals and objectives in the university's strategic plan;
- the underlying objectives for each area of activity in the university, including individual courses of study, areas of research and supporting activities, should be clearly enunciated, so that progress towards their achievement can be assessed;

- the university's organizational structure should be based on devolution of responsibility to its most effective level, accompanied by clear lines of accountability;
- accountability should be ensured by nominating specific monitors for designated activities to report regularly on performance;
- the organizational and financial management of the university should promote managed competition among and within the major academic resource groups;
- methods of allocating funds should provide incentives for improved performance; and
- there should be periodic performance reviews, normally involving external peer assessors, for all academic departments and other major organizational units within the university.

The quality management and assurance plan when it was prepared followed closely the structure of the university's strategic plan. For each of the objectives under each of the goals the relevant procedures for assuring the university on the quality of outcomes relating to that objective were listed and an accountable officer or committee identified as the relevant monitor.

The emphasis of this first plan was very much on process. The university was asked three questions:

- What are we seeking to achieve?
- What procedures do we have in place to assess performance?
- What evidence can we provide to demonstrate our existing achievement and rate improvement?

Outcomes, however, are not neglected in that progress reports of the designated monitors are included in a separate 'Report on progress towards achievement of targets in the strategic plan'. This document is a mixture of descriptive reports, quantitative performance indicators and other statistics and is produced annually at the same time as the university's strategic plan for the forthcoming rolling quinquennium is being reviewed.

The bringing together of the various policy and procedure strands relating to quality assurance within a systematic and structured framework in this way is a significantly beneficial outcome of the focus on quality in higher education.

The university's 1993 quality portfolio

The background, terms of reference and composition of the Committee for Quality Assurance in Higher Education have been described elsewhere. The chair of the Committee was the university's vice-chancellor. Some thought that this gave the university a considerable advantage in handling the preparation of the portfolio and dealing with the audit team's visit. In practice it is believed that it resulted in the vice-chancellor having less involvement in these issues than most other chief executive officers. Brian Wilson was scrupulous in not using his position to advantage his own institution.

The Committee's approach was outlined in a letter to all vice-chancellors towards the end of July 1993. The letter invited institutions to participate in the quality review process and stated:

Those institutions which participate and which are able to demonstrate in the context of their own mission and goals the effectiveness of their quality assurance policies and practices and the excellence of their outcomes, will benefit from a share of the additional funds available for this purpose.

The review process would involve the preparation of a portfolio of quality assurance documentation and evidence of outcomes which would be subject to scrutiny during a one-day visit by one of four review teams established by the Committee.

Enclosed with the letter was a set of guidelines for the 1993 quality assurance programme, one of the attachments to which was a set of guidelines for the preparation of institutional portfolios. The preamble to the guidelines emphasized the voluntary nature of the exercise and how reliant it was on self-evaluation. One of the major omissions from the guidelines was the criteria by which the committee would judge institutional performance. The Committee did not even discuss this matter until after the closing date for submission of portfolios. This was a deliberate ploy to allay any criticism that institutions providing members of the Committee would be advantaged in the preparation of their portfolios.

The Committee had decided to cover in this first review the areas of teaching and learning, research and community service. Each university was required to submit a quality portfolio which it was expected would contain:

- a report of about 15 pages (later increased to 20 pages) reviewing the quality assurance processes and excellence of outcomes and containing an outline of the institution's context, including its mission, objectives, governance, organizational and management structures;
- an appendix incorporating the data used by the institution to demonstrate effectiveness of the quality assurance processes, the quality of outcomes and lists of supplementary documentation which could be made available to the Committee on request.

The guidelines stated that in considering the portfolio the Committee would use the following underlying questions:

- What quality assurance policies and practices does the institution have in place or is developing?
- How effective are these?
- How does the institution judge the quality of its outcomes?
- In what areas and in what ways are the outcomes excellent?
- What are the institution's priorities for improvement?

Although institutions were given only a few weeks to prepare and submit their portfolios, the task at the University of Queensland was not a difficult one in the light of the extensive prior work which had been undertaken. The actual portfolio was drafted by a small group led by the president of the academic board assisted by the secretary and registrar and principal planning officer. Successive drafts were considered by the vice-chancellor's executive, the University Resource and Planning Committee and finally by the university's governing body, the senate. These bodies did little more than polish the initial draft.

The portfolio consisted of a 20-page report under the following headings:

- background and introduction
- mission
- goals
- objectives, targets and strategies
- context
- planning and reporting
- quality management and assurance procedures
- university achievements and evidence for excellence in teaching and learning
- university achievements and evidence for excellence in research and scholarship
- university achievements and evidence for excellence in community and professional service
- major current developments
- priorities for improvement
- documents available on request.

The accompanying 27-page appendix included a list of 40 documents available on request and a series of tables, statistics and other information in support of the portfolio.

In order to keep within the designated guidelines the university was not able to write in very extensive terms on any of the topics. Information was provided largely in note form with cross references to actual documents, statistics and publications.

The portfolio itself contained elements of all of the concepts of quality identified by Harvey *et al.* (1992). The major thrust of the document was to provide evidence of how the university was meeting its mission, goals and objectives *(fitness for purpose)*. The sections on teaching and learning and, in particular, on research focus on the emphasis which is placed on high standards *(excellence)*. A complex and diverse organization such as a university obviously has some difficulty in demonstrating that it can get it right first time and that its output has zero defects, but several sections of the portfolio attempted to demonstrate the way in which the university had successfully maintained high quality outputs over an extended period of years *(consistency)*. The efficiency with which the university pursued its mission and goals was illustrated through a table from the National Report on Australia's Higher Education Sector which showed that the average cost expended on a student completing an undergraduate course at the University of Queensland was the lowest of all the major universities with a similar range of activities, including medicine, dentistry and veterinary science *(value for money)*. Finally, the difficult concept of added value is dealt with in the impressive performance of the university's graduates in finding employment and in the university's research and technology-transfer programmes *(transformation)*.

In perhaps an unusual move (maybe to pre-empt any possibility of legal action) following earlier public criticism, the Committee required institutions, when submitting their quality portfolios, to provide an acknowledgement to the Committee in the following terms:

> I agree to my institution's participation in the quality review process being conducted by the Committee for Quality Assurance in Higher Education and its review teams in accordance with the 1993 Guidelines for Higher Education institutions. I acknowledge that the Committee and its review teams include members of higher education institutions. I also acknowledge that, as advised in the Guidelines for Higher Education Institutions, members of the committee and its review teams are required to absent themselves from consideration by the committee of any matters which relate to their own institutions or those with which they have, or have had, a close association. I agree to my institution's participation on the basis that the Committee and its review teams shall be constituted in accordance with the arrangements acknowledged above.

The 1993 Audit Visit

The final stage of the 1993 review process involved a visit by a review team established by the Committee. The University of Queensland's visit took place on 3 December 1993 and was the last in this initial round. This might have been to the advantage of the university, although hard information about what happened elsewhere was sparse and hard to come by. It was also anticipated that the review team's skills and ability to probe would be well honed. The programme for the day was determined by the review team which interviewed the vice-chancellor (at the beginning and the end of the day) and representatives drawn from the following groups:

- strategic planning sub-committee
- teaching and learning committee
- research and postgraduate studies
- postgraduate students
- undergraduate students
- staff development
- academic staff (levels A-C)
- community service (general)
- community service (links with industry).

Altogether 62 members of staff, students and industrial and community contacts were involved on the day.

One week prior to the visit a mock programme was arranged with two pro-vice-chancellors and the university librarian acting as the review team. This proved invaluable in identifying potential areas of weakness, possible discord and gaps in information. It provided most participants with an experience which turned out to be very close to the actual day itself. The student groups were not involved in this briefing exercise as the university did not wish to be accused of coaching its student responses.

The university is to receive a report from the review team on which it may comment in relation to factual matters and the Committee expects to submit its report to the Minister for Employment, Education and Training in March 1994.

With the possibility of receiving up to 5 per cent of its operating grant (potentially over A$11 million) there is a lot at stake and the university waits with bated breath.

Chapter conclusion

In responding to CQAHE, institutions very obviously tried to respond to criticisms of the sector in the documents we have reviewed; they presented quantitative data about graduation rates and other efficiency measures and data about employment of graduates and similar effectiveness measures. All such measures are open to criticism and challenge if higher education is really concerned with producing graduates who are 'able to form and substantiate independent thought and action in a coherent and articulate fashion' (Barnett, 1992a, p. 58). We will continue to argue that unless all stakeholders try to keep that essential purpose of higher education in view, and try to assess the achievement of that outcome within specific contexts, it is likely that efforts to achieve quality assurance will actually diminish quality. That is not to say, however, that efficiency and effectiveness measures are useless; all kinds of data may inform decision making. Our argument is that we are losing sight of the forest as we focus on the trees in attempting to respond to those stakeholders on whom the institutions depend for their continued existence.

Finally, in an attempt to assure or enhance quality, it is absolutely essential to deal with the issues of responsibility. In the case of higher education, there are shared and mutual responsibilities for the quality of the outcomes, but the processes put in place imply that the universities, and primarily their academic staff, are solely responsible. The one responsibility the universities must not neglect is the responsibility to communicate a clear vision of quality of learning in higher education as transformative and what that means in terms of best practice. It is unrealistic to suggest that universities refuse to play the CQAHE or audit and assessment game, but it is not unrealistic to suggest that in playing it, the universities can help to shift the perspective of those who are making up the rules. In documenting their cases to prove quality learning is being achieved, universities must offer a coherent and consistent vision of what constitutes high quality learning, what conditions foster it and how to assess it.

Chapter 3

Challenges to Higher Education

Throughout our summary of the pressures for reform, change and quality assurance, we see many challenges being hurled at higher education. A substantial conflict underlies attempts to meet those challenges: the tension between demands by the various stakeholders for accountability, public disclosure and their right to influence the system including curriculum, and a tradition of academic professionalism which has always assumed that the autonomy of academics protects the system and ensures intellectual freedom.

Being professional and accountable

The profession of being an academic is, in itself, a double-barrelled challenge in that one is expected to be fully initiated into one's discipline – as a scholar and researcher and someone who shares the ethos as well as the methods of the discipline. One is also expected to be able to operate as a professional educator and increasingly there is recognition that initiation into the discipline does not guarantee professionalism as a teacher. Consequently, a number of institutions are now offering postgraduate programmes in higher education for academics who are already highly qualified professionals in their disciplines. (See Pennington's case study in this chapter or Andresen, 1991, for a description of the programme offered at the University of New South Wales.) Some institutions emphasize non-award professional development activities for academics. (See Taylor's case study in Chapter 4 for example.) Some offer both formal programmes of study and non-award professional development simultaneously, as at the University of New South Wales.

In response to demands for accountability, academics can argue that they do expose their work – as teachers and as researchers – more publicly than most workers. Statements about teaching being 'an activity conducted in private between not always consenting adults' (Elton, 1993, p.134) misrepresent the activity as we know it. When one enters a classroom there is an audience – a very critical one – and very few teachers can dismiss or ignore the unmistakable signs when one is failing to achieve one's goals; no one wants to fail publicly over and over again. In addition to the student audience, teachers in higher education are open to further scrutiny: the public has access to their classrooms, their course materials and to their publications; the public can obtain course proposals through minutes of academic boards (or equivalent bodies); course materials and examination papers are available in university libraries; some courses are even broadcast on television in open learning programmes; government funding bodies publish lists of successful applications for funding and frequently publish reports of academic research commissioned by government; and so on.

Indeed, the encouragement to prepare a professional portfolio of the type described by Pennington in his case study is another response to demands for accountability being taken by many institutions. Materials compiled range over activities such as teaching, research, administration, professional renewal, community service and so on, (see O'Neil and Pennington, 1992) in a critical way, adhering to the ethos of a 'reflective practitioner' (Schön, 1983, 1987). It is more than a mere listing of activities as in a *curriculum vitae*; it is a compilation of intentions, strategic actions and reflections and it covers the creative elements of being an academic as well as the routine.

Growth without resources

Other challenges to higher education include those associated with moving from an élite to a mass higher education system. Growth in higher education has already been quite astounding. In Australia, where the population has scarcely doubled since 1952, the number of students in higher education has increased by a factor of 13. In 1952 the number of graduates for the year was 4,304; in 1992 it was expected to be 100,000 (HEC, 1992c). Obviously the mix of backgrounds of students must be broader than it was 40 years ago, but there is still evidence that the students attending universities are disproportionately from relatively privileged white English-speaking backgrounds. The challenge is to increase access for those students who have not traditionally attended university and then to provide equitable opportunities for them to succeed. This goal challenges not only student support systems – financial, counselling, study skills advisers – but also curriculum design and classroom teaching methods. It also challenges the system to find alternative ways of selecting students for admission when they have not jumped all of the traditional hoops, ways of granting advanced standing to students who have studied in further education or in the workplace and ways of recognizing and granting credit for learning through experience rather than formal study. Finally, no matter how strongly supported is the goal of increased access, there is a challenge to the quality of higher education which must be taken seriously and cannot be dismissed simply as the élitism of those who defend 'standards' without being able to define them.

The challenge to quality posed by demands for more growth is exacerbated by the substantial decline in the unit of resource. In Australia from 1983 to 1991, dollars per effective full-time student unit (EFTSU) declined by 16.3 per cent. Although there should be an improvement by 1994, dollars per EFTSU will still be 8 per cent below 1983 levels (HEC, 1992c, p.40). In 1992 (and for several years previous) student:staff ratios in Australian higher education have been above those in secondary schools. Expenditure on education as a proportion of GDP is falling, from 5.6 per cent in 1982–3 to 4.7 per cent in 1989–90, and a predicted 3.6–3.9 per cent in 2001 (HEC, 1992c, p.40). Various bodies have reported substantial shortfalls in funding for construction and maintenance of buildings, replacement of antiquated equipment and provision of adequate library resources.

Maintaining quality with further growth is also challenged by shortages of appropriately qualified people willing to accept positions in universities. Our experience suggests that this is true of general staff as well as academic, but the official data document impending shortages of academics as those appointed in the last growth period retire and the 'production' of PhDs cannot meet demand. Some disciplines already face great difficulty in recruitment and are forced to pay incentive salaries (which the department and institution can ill afford) and/or to hire staff of non-English speaking backgrounds. Regardless of their educational qualifications – usually very good – the difficulties of language cannot be overestimated. One staff developer in Australia reported being asked to assist a group of new junior academic staff with small-group teaching techniques and discovering that there were 14 different language backgrounds in a group of 18 and that they had difficulty not only with the cultural assumptions of what it means to lead a small interactive group but also with the exigencies of communicating with their students, each other, subject coordinators and other colleagues.

Since there seems to be little hope that the funding shortfalls will be made up from government coffers, the institutions are under pressure to find alternative sources of funding. Some of the richer can afford to appoint professional fund-raisers, but even in those institutions academic staff are under constant pressure to 'be entrepreneurial', another task added to their informal job-descriptions at a time when they are also dealing with more students with fewer technical and clerical support staff. Yet another challenge to quality.

Maintaining diversity and purpose

With the end of the binary systems in both the United Kingdom and Australia there is a challenge to retain diversity in the system. The espoused theory is that it is in everyone's best interests to have diversity and choice in the system; that there are many stakeholders with many differing needs which can only be addressed if institutions establish and retain their individual identities. The theory in practice seems to have a different goal. Although there was a great deal of research, including 'pure' research, being done in colleges and polytechnics before the reform of the system, they were not expected to compete with the universities on the basis of their success in research – obtaining funding and achieving outcomes. Now they are and from the other side, at least in Australia and the UK, there is to be competition in teaching which will affect funding levels as well. All are being called upon to readjust balances between teaching and research. The danger is that there will be a drift towards uniform mediocrity as everyone tries to be all things to all stakeholders.

Perhaps the most challenging challenge of all to higher education is to be responsive to the various stakeholders without sacrificing the essential nature of higher education. In reporting on a project on *Learning Outcomes in Higher Education* for the Unit for Development of Adult Continuing Education (now merged with the Further Education Unit), Sue Otter (1992) reports on the differences in perspective of employers and academics and students when they are asked about the outcomes they value. Employers and academics agree in large part on the 'core' outcomes, such as communication and problem-solving skills, but employers did not value the subject-specific outcomes which were very important to the academics, and students tended to emphasize outcomes related to personal development (such as gaining self-esteem). The issue is not who is right but what might happen to vital functions of higher education other than preparing the workforce for employment if the autonomy of the institutions is not preserved and the professionalism of their staff is not recognized. While permanent residence in ivory towers cannot be defended, it would be a pity if they were all torn down and there was no quiet place of refuge for those who may still advance frontiers of knowledge if all of the other demands on their time can be accommodated.

Loss of the stable state

Writing in 1971 of the loss of the stable state throughout all sectors of Western society, Schön described the pressures on universities:

> Universities have found themselves under conflicting pressures. Government urges them to assume new national and regional roles for which they are ill-prepared and with which their traditional ideals of scholarship and liberal education conflict. Students press for redistribution of power and for education more relevant to the world outside. The university is set conflicting goals, in preparing students for

particular vocations, keeping its own financial autonomy and responding to growing demands for higher education. The functions of education and the role of the university in our society seem hopelessly confused. (Schön, 1971, p.19)

Schön argues that as a result of rapid change on all fronts and the complexity of social systems, correcting problems cannot be achieved by diagnosing the mismatch between problems and the approaches of discrete institutions. The mismatch is at a higher level; it is a result of the system failing to address the problems. 'But in our society public learning has been limited to the transformation of specific organisations. Broad functional systems transform themselves through slow and uncertain chain reactions' (p.183). In tracing the evolution of government policy, we have documented the uncertainty of one such chain reaction.

Schön emphasizes the problems of trying to reform a whole system. Since it is impossible to invade or overthrow an institution/system which has no embodiment, and since it is also undesirable to threaten perpetual disruption,

The creation of a new functional system combining many previous separate components leads chiefly to two fundamentally different strategies:

- Gain control of all elements of the functional system in order to subject them to central management.
- Knit together the still autonomous elements of the functional system in networks which permit concerted action. (Schön, 1971, p.183)

The need for networks

We have seen that different stakeholders have identified different problems and solutions for higher education. Some would see the approaches of governments as attempts to follow the first of Schön's strategies, but the nature of universities and the interplay of other stakeholders seems to make it extremely unlikely that such a strategy will succeed. The alternative of a network serving 'as a kind of "shadow system" for the creation of [a] functional system' (p.194) is not only more desirable and appropriate to the enterprise of higher education, it is also possible. The 'shadow network' fills the gap between the fragmented groups of stakeholders and a more highly aggregated functional system, the design of which is unimaginable.

The need for networks to address society's problems in the unstable state of contemporary existence makes new demands on individuals. They must take on new roles such as negotiator, broker, facilitator, 'underground' manager, network manager (see Schön, 1971, pp.197–200). These are uncomfortable roles which place individuals at personal risk and which require great personal credibility among groups with differing values and goals. Often people involved in sustaining networks exist on the margins of a number of institutions. Schön reminds us that there are both negative and positive connotations to being at the margins. One may not be central and may be excluded but one may also be at the forefront – few dramatic changes have been instituted from the centre of any organization without some irresistible pressure from outside or from a fringe-dweller.

With the loss of the stable state we see the failure of the rational/ experimental model of public inquiry (Schön, 1971, Chapter 7). Trying rationally to collect and analyse data in order to make predictions about future events is a futile exercise when, because of the rapidity of change, the data are insufficient before they are analysed; when because of the complexity of the systems, there is too much information to be comprehended and too many perspectives from which it may be viewed; and when because the system will have already changed, prediction on the basis of the past must be disproved.

Schön develops a portrait of a 'learning agent' who may be an individual but which may be a group or organization which is able to develop projective models as they move from situation to situation, developing models of situation-action-and-effect. These agents tolerate the ambiguity and overload of information and learn from action and experience; they are not surprised by the unexpected because they accept the open-endedness of all situations. Though there is no prediction in the old experimental science sense, there is continuity in the learning process provided by the 'social memory' of the learning agent. These learning agents are not immobilized by instability:

> The learning agent must be willing and able to make the leaps required in existential knowledge. These are the leaps from informational overload to the first formulation of the problem, from an absence of theory to convergence on a design for public action, and from the experience of one situation to its use as a projective model in the next instance. These are leaps, because they cannot be justified except by what happens after they are made. They are conditions, not consequences, of knowledge. (Schön, 1971, p.235)

We believe that the approach to improving higher education which we propose in the following chapters will encourage more people to become learning agents and to address constructively the loss of a stable state within the system of higher education. The following case study includes some strategies for improving teaching and learning which will facilitate the formation of networks and the development of learning agents.

CASE STUDY

Developing Learning Agents

Gus Pennington, University of Teesside

Few observers of the higher education scene in the UK can doubt that the issue of quality in teaching and learning has, in a relatively short period, assumed increased significance at both a local and national level. Since the well-researched but ultimately disappointing Warnock Report (1990) on quality in higher education (see Colling, 1993) a crop of national initiatives have offered institutions opportunities (often on a competitive bidding basis) to participate in a range of programmes aimed at the improvement of university teaching. In a context of rising student numbers and resource constraints, such initiatives have tended to focus on what a variety of agencies perceive to be national priorities requiring some form of focused practical action:

- Employment Department: Enterprise in Higher Education programme encourages reform to develop transferable, work-related skills alongside specialist subject knowledge (see Macnair, 1990; Wright, 1992);
- Royal Society of Arts: Higher Education for Capability has similar objectives (see Stephenson and Weil, 1992);
- Polytechnics and Colleges Funding Council: Teaching More Students project addresses problems of rapid expansion (see Gibbs, 1992c);
- Higher Education Funding Council (HEFC): Teaching and Learning Technology Programme encourages consortia of universities to enhance student learning through technology.

These activities have sensitized institutions to curriculum change and exposed a wider audience of academics to discussions centred on teaching quality, educational effectiveness and resource efficiency. These discussions have been further sharpened by activities associated with quality auditing of institutional structures and visits by HEFCE assessors to determine the quality of teaching at subject level. The net result of all these pressures has been to place teaching in a more prominent position on everyone's agenda, though the tension between priorities for research and for teaching in higher education is still a source of frictional heat.

This case study describes the steps the University of Teesside has taken to establish a set of activities which contribute to a professional development programme for academic staff.

The professional development programme (PDP)

The strategy for quality enhancement of teaching and learning consists of three interrelated elements:

- provision of a mandatory, two-semester, part-time course for academic staff which leads to the award of a postgraduate certificate in teaching and learning in higher education (first offered in this form in 1991);
- provision of a voluntary, project-based programme for experienced staff employing cycles of action research which leads to the award of a postgraduate diploma (first offered in 1992);
- introduction of an 'Improvement of Teaching' scheme involving direct classroom observation and feedback on a peer basis (first begun on a pilot basis with two university schools in 1993).

The educational development service (EDS) in the university, consisting of four full-time members of academic staff, has been responsible for the development and delivery of each of these elements and this has resulted in a number of outcomes:

- Each type of provision has been designed to the same set of operational principles; ie, it must emphasize the development of competence and activities must be clearly work-based and rooted in the normal tasks of teaching staff. The role of the EDS is to support improvement as a collegial activity, to increase 'know-how' of teaching and produce competent 'reflective practitioners'.
- Each type of provision uses learning contracts as a means of identifying outcomes and responsibilities. As an incidental by-product of their use of these, staff are more favourably inclined to adopt them with students.
- Each type of provision employs a portfolio as a diagnostic, developmental and evaluative 'tool'. This too creates a climate in which academics are more amenable to the use of student portfolios and gain familiarity with portfolio-based assessment – an important ingredient for the assessment of prior learning and the adoption of National Vocational Qualifications (NVQs).
- A team approach has enabled us to increase the coherence of the separate elements and to make 'efficiency' gains in terms of the methods and materials deployed. This latter point is particularly important as we need to manage the professional development programme with other work entailing individual and group consultancy, course evaluations (some 40–50 each academic year), committee and course validation work, and inputs to strategic thinking in the university.

The post graduate certificate (PGC): background

The university (then polytechnic) had established its own in-house certificate in teaching in the mid-1980s in recognition of the need to make formal provision for new staff with little or no teaching experience.

In the late 1980s the higher education environment changed considerably and teaching staff, both new and experienced, were subjected to an increasing set of demands arising from an accumulation of developments. The widening of access created quantitative and qualitative changes in working practices which tested lecturers' capabilities; and demands for new forms of assessment and an emphasis on work-related skills added further to the dynamic nature of the HE curriculum. Programme redesign, the continuous improvement of curriculum practice and a greater variety in course delivery methods became standard features of academic work. These internal pressures interacted with the kinds of national initiatives already identified to produce a climate which began to stress professionalism in teaching, effectiveness in learning and the maintenance of curriculum relevance without loss of rigour. Within this context by 1990 we had recognized that the original certificate, while useful, had begun to need the kind of overhaul and redesign that most other programmes had undergone.

Student feedback (from more than 600 students per year located in more than 40 courses) revealed four major weaknesses in the university's taught programmes:

- the need for more effective teaching delivery (50 per cent of student comments);
- the need for greater coherence in assessment methods (23 per cent);
- the need for better course management and design (16 per cent);
- other factors (11 per cent).

Academics' concerns were with:

- active learning method;
- development and use of portfolios;
- generic skills development;
- assessing more students;
- teaching large classes;
- assessment of competences;
- independent learning;
- self- and peer assessment;
- group-working skills;
- improving course quality.

Our experience in running the certificate and this information provided a clear pointer to the direction in which we needed to move and reinforced our overall aspiration to provide a programme which 'developed academic staffs' ability to perform confidently and competently in classroom and other learning environments', by equipping them 'with the skills and understanding necessary for effective teaching practice and the support of student learning' (PGC course document, 1992).

The new certificate

This element of the PDP is delivered on a modular basis and involves a notional minimum of some 270 study hours, approximately half of which are delivered face-to-face. Structurally, the certificate is broken into four free-standing modules, two of which are delivered in each 15-week semester of the academic year. Units of study are built around four major organizing themes:

- the role of the teacher in HE and the elements of effective teaching;

- issues in and approaches to assessment;
- the management of effective learning – the students' experience;
- issues in curriculum development and approaches to evaluation.

Each theme has a negotiated assignment attached to it and this work is grounded in participants' *actual* teaching activities. Thus, for example, during the module on assessment staff will work on the assessment and assignment demands of their teaching at that particular time and devise appropriate essay titles, marking schemes and feedback procedures – each with its accompanying rationale. Some flexibility is necessary to make this approach work and the use of learning contracts (see Stephenson and Laycock, 1993) is a device employed to control a situation which might become anarchic. Participants generally like this approach as it:

- integrates 'theory' and 'practice';
- formalizes (and improves!) activities they would have had to undertake anyway;
- accelerates learning and familiarizes them with the use of a learning contract if they subsequently wish to use this approach with students.

As the programme progresses the interactive nature of the four basic themes becomes more apparent and participants gradually begin to recognize that each is merely a 'point of entry' to the complexities of classroom life.

Certificate operational issues   During the first semester, course contact time is deliberately high – some three hours each week plus a tutorial and direct observation of teaching with feedback. Our view is that new staff need high levels of support initially to build confidence and competence. Great store is placed on development of a 'critical practice' which while accepting the realities of participants' contexts, nevertheless attempts to model good practice and to establish a 'best fit' between the given reality and an idealized standard. Throughout, the style of operation is one of the EDS working with new colleagues as critical friends and quasi-consultants. In this way the programme soon comes to be perceived as a direct contribution to normal daily work rather than an unwelcome additional demand. Our experience to date confirms the efficacy of this approach to professional development which 'resides essentially in working *with,* not working *on* people' (Lieberman, 1986).

A wide range of teaching methods are employed to deliver the programme, including lectures, seminars, tutorials, workshops, peer feedback, demonstrations, case studies and simulations. In designing the course we worked to match teaching-learning methods to the kind of outcomes we were seeking and to model certain approaches in order to allow participants to experience them *as learners* before looking at their potential as lecturers. We believe that it is important for participants to make judgements about the appropriateness of particular teaching and learning approaches in terms of local contexts, their subject disciplines and the traditions operating amongst their own course teams. So while always seeking best practice, we are prepared to be pragmatic – better that a colleague performs well in a preferred, possibly narrow, range of activities than poorly across a wider range prescribed by others.

This tradition of making your own judgement is, of course, sometimes perceived to be 'fence-sitting', particularly during the early days of the programme when some participants would like to be told the 'answers'. Our view, however, is that it is important to establish early that learning how to teach is a process which never ends (cf. Ramsden, 1992) and that our approach is a precursor to developing the kind of 'reflective practitioner' higher education needs if the sector it is to manage waves of curriculum renewal and a self-regulated approach to quality in teaching. A second point is that this approach is necessary in political terms in that the EDS works essentially through influence and consent. Since our mission includes evaluation *and* developmental activities, it is advantageous to establish that expertise in teaching is not the monopoly of a single group and that many styles are permissible, providing they are effective. Deploying expertise without prescription is the essence of facilitative development and underwrites our acceptance in all corners of the campus.

A major innovation in the new postgraduate certificate has been the adoption of a teaching portfolio as a major integrative mechanism. Each participant is provided with such a document at the beginning of the programme and this is added to as activities progress. The initial purpose of the portfolio is diagnostic and participants 'audit' their existing skills a number of times against prepared profiles as a preliminary to tutorial contacts. As the programme advances the nature of the portfolio changes; it becomes more interactive, developmental and cumulative in the sense that assignments and observational feedback are interleaved with other materials. In the final part of the programme the portfolio becomes a major vehicle for reflection and, ultimately, for assessment in that it is this document which is considered by internal and external examiners as evidence of participants' capabilities to perform against our expected programme outcomes. The portfolio evidence demonstrates that participants are able to:

- design and deliver a coherent teaching programme;
- use a range of teaching and learning methods and select methods appropriate to desired learning outcomes;
- develop and use a variety of teaching aids;
- employ a range of techniques to assess students' work and match these to intended learning outcomes;
- perform effectively as a personal tutor;
- monitor and evaluate their own teaching performances and evaluate programmes they deliver;
- reflect upon their own teaching practice, identify needs and form plans for continuing development.

Certificate outcomes   Evaluations to date indicate that the programme is broadly achieving its objectives and that participants develop significantly over a 30-week period. New staff are particularly enthusiastic about the direct observation of their teaching and the feedback provided by EDS tutors. This element is proving to be a powerful mechanism for improvement and we have increased the observational element despite it being 'resource intensive'. Our interim judgement is that the new certificate is working well because:

- the programme acknowledges and is congruent with participants' work tasks;
- the teaching team from the EDS have a common set of understandings and values which underpin programme delivery;
- teaching materials have been developed jointly and produced to a high standard in 'unit' packs – this ensures coherence, continuity and conformance to an agreed template;
- the programme is a contractual requirement for new, inexperienced members of staff – this is indicated during the interview stage of the selection procedures and all newly appointed staff received details of the programme with their letter of appointment;
- during their first year of teaching all course participants are given a weekly remission from their teaching load to attend the programme – this signals clearly the schools' and institution's commitment to staff involvement;
- subject groupings undergoing quality assessment point to participation in the programme as an element in their quality enhancement strategies;
- course participants act as advocates for educational development and help to create a local climate more susceptible to subsequent consultancy.

The postgraduate diploma: philosophy

The diploma, like the certificate, is a part-time course but is offered to experienced teaching staff with at least three years' experience in higher education or those who possess a recognized teaching qualification. Its aim is to provide a tutor-supported opportunity for staff systematically to investigate problems and issues in their own professional practice with a view to making their performance more effective. The programme is project-based and entails completion of three action research reports (with associated materials) within a flexible time frame of not less than 12 and not more than 24 months.

The philosophy, structure and methods underpinning the course are drawn from three major sources each of which emphasizes the notion of 'teacher-as-researcher'. These are:

- theoretical perspectives generated in the UK by educationalists such as Bell (1988), Revans (1982) and Stenhouse (1983);
- theoretical perspectives and descriptions of practice from Australia such as Kemmis (1988) and Zuber-Skerritt (1990, 1992a, 1992b); and

■ 'grounded theory' as research methodology (Glaser and Strauss, 1967).

In designing the course the EDS was very much drawn to two quotations from this literature and used these as guiding principles to inform the development process. These were:

> Action research is critical enquiry by reflecting practitioners into their own practice with a view to problem solving and continual development of themselves and their practice. Zuber-Skerritt (1990)

> Action research is based on the fundamental concept of experiential learning. People work on the real issues of relevance to themselves and co-workers, for which they carry real responsibility. Revans (1982)

For us, the action research approach enabled the EDS to bring together four important objectives, namely:

■ a theory of learning to underpin continuing professional development;
■ a methodology for quality enhancement;
■ a mechanism for generating examples of good practice to disseminate to a wider internal audience;
■ a means for accrediting the professional expertise of experienced staff.

Diploma operational issues   Entry to the diploma programme is normally through the production and assessment of a portfolio which draws together a variety of forms of evidence to demonstrate that the prospective participant is already a 'competent practitioner'. Discussion with EDS tutors enables individuals to identify evidence of their capabilities and encourages first attempts to articulate a philosophy of education and to comment on their theories of teaching and learning. Thus, compiling the portfolio begins the process of reflection which is central to the projects themselves (cf. Boud *et al.*, 1985b). Spending time on discussion places value on the experience and knowledge participants bring with them. It also encourages them to:

■ take stock of existing activities and behaviours;
■ record (and assess) their career to date;
■ develop a sense of emerging needs;
■ begin planning for their projects (cf. Harrison, 1993).

After an initial short taught module which critically examines assumptions underlying the methodology of action research, the 'content' of the programme is driven by participants' own interests. The particular focus of each project is negotiated and governed by a learning contract describing:

■ the objectives of the inquiry;
■ the intended outcomes;
■ agreed methods and an agreed calendar;

■ the criteria for assessment.

Agreeing the learning contract is an important stage for both the participants and ourselves. It represents the 'blueprint' for the project, a commitment to work together and a framework for monitoring progress. Our experience suggests that investing time and energy at this stage is important for success. As the contract evolves, participants will typically be expected to:

■ review the current state of affairs in their chosen teaching-learning context;
■ identify and analyse factors affecting the situation;
■ decide whether changes are necessary and if so, describe and justify what these should be;
■ undertake a viable programme of action which acknowledges such factors as time-scale, the sequencing of tasks and resource implications – in order subsequently to:
■ report on the evaluated outcomes of action and to draw conclusions grounded in relevant literature and professional debate.

Participants may opt for three equally weighted projects or for a major and minor topic. This choice acknowledges the differing scale of issues participants wish to engage with and also allows for collaborative work. The latter is actively encouraged by the course team as we believe it mirrors the kind of peer support needed to sustain curriculum change on a broad front and it avoids the debilitating factors associated with lone, 'heroic innovators' acting in isolation. During the first cycle of operation typical projects have included:

■ evaluation of the experience of student peer assessment in a major group project;
■ production of a guided self-study pack for a social science statistical package;
■ design of a self-administered diagnostic test for information technology skills;
■ development of a curriculum for work-based learning;
■ computer aided assessment in accountancy;
■ the introduction of learning contracts in a business communication course;
■ use of a student-produced video to improve presentational skills.

Diploma outcomes   Interim feedback on the programme is positive and we are receiving more approaches from experienced staff for admission. We see the benefits of our approach as follows:

■ established academics are actively exposed through the course processes to the use of portfolios and learning contracts with a view to their later adoption with students;
■ the potential tension between teaching and research is reduced – staff can improve their teaching *and* research profile at the same time by researching aspects of their teaching practice;

- by the end of the programme participants have at least three potential publications which can be used for other purposes (eg, research selectivity exercises, quality assessment, promotion);
- a stock of in-house examples of effective practice are generated for use with others;
- through time, a group of 'reflective practitioners' is created which is interested in the practicalities of teaching but which examines these in a rigorous, self-critical manner;
- staff are easily able to provide convincing evidence of their commitment to teaching and their level of performance in the context of appraisal.

The 'Improvement of Teaching' scheme

Direct observation of teaching is considered to be an important element in the university's procedures for quality assurance and quality enhancement. It complements a range of existing practices associated with induction, the institutional staff development and review scheme (SDR), capability procedures to test satisfactory levels of performance and the kinds of 'front-line' quality control operated by course leaders and programme managers. Observation with peer feedback also helps the university to fill a long-standing gap in its quality procedures by providing supplementary information to lay alongside data from student feedback at course and module level.

The decision to move ahead with the scheme was not an easy one given the sensitivities surrounding the issues and the UK government's recent stance on performance-related pay. This being the case, during initial discussion with senior managers the EDS advised that resistance might be reduced by stressing:

- the intrinsically strong rationale for its introduction as an element in a strategic approach to quality improvement in teaching;
- the scheme generates reliable data for self-assessment exercises (both internal and external);
- that initial involvement would be on the basis of a pilot study which would enable the university to evaluate staff's responses, to refine and adapt the training procedures and documentation;
- that selection of staff for involvement in the pilot phase would be on a voluntary basis;
- the lack of any intention to create a permanent 'official' cadre of observers and an assurance that the observational process would be owned and managed locally by subject groupings themselves – there would be no 'visiting experts';
- that observation linked to peer feedback provides *mutual* benefits to the parties involved and that an important secondary outcome is the development of a larger staff group with reviewing and feedback skills of relevance to their work with students and with additional transfer to the wider working environment.

The role of the EDS in developing the scheme was an interesting one and illustrates the need for educational developers to move with a degree of nimbleness between the needs of institutional managers and teaching colleagues. During the development phases we:

- produced briefing papers and suggested operational principles;
- liaised with and briefed senior managers, deans, personnel staff and union representatives;
- presented papers at committees concerned with academic policy and academic standards;
- produced guidelines for practice and training materials;
- ran workshops for observers.

The result of these procedures has been generally positive and although the EDS would like to claim some responsibility for persuasive advocacy, acceptance has obviously been stimulated in part by the demands of HEFCE quality assessment and the impending site visits of subject assessors. Although it is too soon to identify any clear outcomes (training is taking place during the writing of this case study), we have been able to establish a number of agreed operational principles, namely that:

- the scheme is developmental in character and intentions – the main aim is to help staff, particularly in a time of rapid change, to reflect critically upon their teaching through planned and systematic observation, reflection and mutual analysis. Feedback from observation frequently stimulates staff to try out new ideas, reaffirms what is effective in existing practice and helps modify current techniques. All these processes help to improve the quality of students' learning;
- it is separated from recent initiatives to introduce merit pay by operating on a different time phase to pay negotiations and involves individuals as observers who will not normally participate in a formal reviewing role for SDR purposes;
- the effectiveness of the scheme is to a large extent dependent on the use of a professional portfolio by academic staff and that data in an individual's portfolio are owned by them, indeed *they* are responsible for decisions regarding their selection, collation, presentational format and deployment;
- observers will receive training for their role and that at least two but no more than three observations will be conducted in any one academic year. Furthermore, it is desirable that these observations cover a range of different teaching formats (eg, lectures, small-group work, practicals);
- documentation will be kept of the observation, subsequent feedback and any resulting action and outcomes;
- all data generated through observation are confidential to the individuals concerned and shall not be used for purposes other than the improvement of professional practice.

Concluding remarks

While each of these elements make their own contribution to the enhancement of teaching, when aggregated they have the potential to generate a significant 'multiplier effect'. The strategy has been that over a period of three years the EDS would provide opportunities for different groupings of academic staff to undertake a variety of forms of professional development suited to their needs and in delivery formats they find attractive and useful. Our intention has also been to move away from a menu-driven approach to professional development based essentially on short workshops to other forms of support which are more continuous, rooted in work practices and consultancy led. Provision of these three major elements (certificate, diploma and observation) has helped us with the perennial problem of training and development units, namely, striking an appropriate balance between institutional *presence* (many small discrete events) and institutional *impact* (fewer activities, greater congruence and more depth).

At the same time we have recognized that these initiatives *by themselves*, even when aggregated, will have less impact than intended unless they are rooted in an institutional culture which values learning for both students *and* staff. Indeed, we believe that the creation of the 'learning organization' is the ultimate goal of any individual or unit charged with a developmental function (Senge, 1990). This being so, the EDS is attempting to facilitate a more broadly based appreciation that 'teaching and learning take place in a complex, interacting *system*' and that 'the outcomes of learning depend on the combined effects of the whole environment' (McFarlane, 1992).

Thus, in conjunction with the initiatives described here, the university is also progressing a series of congruent strategies which support the development of IT for teaching and learning across the campus, and the widespread improvement of the physical learning environment. Developing the teaching competence of academic staff obviously coheres with these other policies and recognizes the need to manage broadly-based organizational change composed of interlocking behavioural, attitudinal, procedural and structural elements. Features being established to ensure wider quality and indicate that effective teaching is valued include:

- transmission of clear messages about the centrality of teaching and learning to prospective staff and students during the recruitment process (cf. The Students Charter initiative in the UK);
- adoption of selection mechanisms for academic staff which test the candidate's philosophy, motivation and practices regarding teaching;
- provision of mandatory educational development programmes for *all* staff which stress professional proficiency, role competence and skill acquisition – this would include part-time staff, research assistants and in some cases technicians;
- establishment of reward structures and promotion criteria which acknowledge excellence in teaching – this would include the conferment of professorships for excellence in teaching;

- adoption of a teaching portfolio for *all* members of the academic staff to be deployed during appraisal, review and promotion interviews;
- creation of a faculty base for coordinating and disseminating good practice in teaching and learning, including the possibility of having part-time faculty coordinators for the development of teaching and learning;
- development of a detailed teaching and learning strategy and the linking of this to the institutional development plan;
- establishment of mechanisms actively to encourage and fund innovations in teaching and learning;
- creation of a forum(s) in which there is collective discussion by staff of good teaching practice;
- and finally, the location of an educational development unit and its staff within an organizational structure which aligns its contribution and mission to the academic activities associated with quality assurance and quality improvement.

This case study describes one institution's practice but raises larger questions about the kind of stance institutions generally ought to be adopting towards issues of quality in teaching and learning if we are to see measurable improvements during the coming decade. The choice options might be described as follows; do we adopt:

- a short-term contingent approach or a long-term strategic engagement with quality?
- a compliant and minimalist approach or a self-critical and developmental one?
- a periodic and incrementalist approach or ongoing coherent engagement?
- a regulatory stance or one committed to continuous improvement?

Educational developers must engage with quality enhancement – they have no option – and their major role is perhaps best described as helping to create a culture in which individuals and groups move progressively from the left-hand choice position towards the right-hand one.

Chapter 4

Characteristics of Quality Learning

We take the overarching purpose of higher education to be fostering higher order intellectual capacities in students. A general statement of what those capacities allow students to do is that when they possess them, students can 'form and substantiate independent thought and action in a coherent and articulate fashion' (Barnett, 1992a, p.58). The purpose of a university education is thus about developing general qualities of a personal and social kind as well as those of an intellectual kind. It encompasses outcomes including communication skills, problem-solving abilities, interpersonal skills, planning and strategic thinking abilities and critical and evaluative skills, including logic. It seems necessary to expand on this general statement to some extent in order to characterize what, in our view, high quality learning actually is. In the following discussion of the characteristics of high quality learning, we use the term 'knowledge' with some reservations.

We hope that our readers will think of the different types of knowing appropriate to their own disciplines as they consider whether our characterization of high quality learning in general fits their understanding of what such learning is in their own context. We sought an ordinary word, but the trouble with ordinary words is that they carry a lot of baggage and it is important to make sure that we are not picking up someone else's portmanteau inadvertently. Too often the word 'knowledge' is associated only with facts, with the content of disciplines which has dominated higher education curriculum planning and pedagogy (see Barnett, 1992a; Biggs, 1989; Gibbs, 1992b, for developed argument on this point). To emphasize that theory does not necessarily lead to practice, a distinction has been made between 'knowing that' and 'knowing how'; we use the word 'knowledge' to mean both of these. Thus, referring back to Barnett's statement of the overarching purpose, knowledge is about both thought and action; we use the word to represent knowledge of facts, of relations, of operations, of methodologies and so on. It is a portmanteau word; we will unpack it in the following pages.

The characteristics of high quality learning

High quality learning is characterized by being able to discover knowledge for oneself.

The learner is not a sponge soaking up information which has already been processed by a single instructor. He or she has research skills and the ability to analyse and synthesize the material she or he gathers, be it quantitative or verbal. In addition, she or he is critical enough to continue to question conclusions. She or he understands different learning strategies and can choose the most appropriate for the task at hand. Being able to discover knowledge for oneself does not necessarily mean that the knowledge must be new to the whole world, as in the 'original contribution' of a PhD thesis; it simply means discovering something new to the learner.

High quality learning is characterized by long-term retention of the knowledge.

Even when it comes to remembering facts, names, formulae, etc., the evidence is that an approach to learning emphasizing understanding rather than memorization results in greater retention (Gibbs, 1992b, p.153). However, retention does not imply failure to question or unwillingness to change thoughts and actions when there is sufficient evidence to require one to do so.

High quality learning is characterized by being able to perceive relations between old knowledge and new.

The learner cannot disregard past experience. The ideas and methodologies of one area of study should inform others. The quality learner is always trying to put the pieces together, to apply logic.

High quality learning is characterized by being able to create new knowledge.

This goes beyond being independent in discovering knowledge in that it is creative, but the newly created knowledge may still be old to someone else. Independently discovering what others have learned and documented, perceiving the relations between that knowledge and one's own experiences and previous learning and developing new insights would be one example of creating new knowledge, even though someone else had arrived at the same insight previously.

High quality learning is characterized by being able to apply one's knowledge to solving problems.

Obviously these characteristics overlap. For instance, putting the pieces of data, information, experience, etc. together is necessary to solving problems. The importance of stating this characteristic is to make specific the value we attach to acting as well as thinking. Interpersonal skills come into play in much problem-solving.

High quality learning is characterized by being able to communicate one's knowledge to others.

Barnett says the learner must form and *substantiate* independent thought and action in a coherent and *articulate* fashion. Communication of knowledge almost always requires the spoken and/or written word, but it may also require skills of numeracy, skills in graphical representation, technical drawing, musical notation, sculpting, etc., etc. And, here too, interpersonal skills are a factor, as well as logic.

High quality learning is characterized by one's wanting to know more.

Enabling people to become lifelong learners has become part of the educational buzz (see Duke, 1992): high quality learning requires one to go on with the task because it requires one to be questioning and critical, of self and of one's environment.

High quality learning is characterized by all of the above. Thus, it is not high quality learning to locate an anatomy text and identify all of the nerves in the human shoulder, check with other texts that there is no controversy about these names, memorize them and reel them off in a test if, for instance, one promptly forgets the names, or fails to locate a specific nerve in relation to a specific muscle studied the week before, or does not wish to understand the function of the nerve. One may not immediately apply the knowledge, but one would be able to if one were engaged in a programme of study – self-imposed or designed by someone else – which led to high quality learning. That brings us to consider the conditions under which high quality learning is likely to occur. We believe each of these conditions to be necessary; none is sufficient.

The conditions necessary for high quality learning

As we review the pressures – both external and internal – on higher education to become more visibly and systematically concerned with quality, and quality in teaching in particular, we are struck by some of the relatively simplistic assumptions about what will achieve this quality revolution. For instance, employ a performance indicator revealing the ratio of graduates to entrants to degree programmes to allow efficient institutions to be rewarded for their good performance. Or survey graduates and/or their employers to determine their satisfaction with the outputs of the universities. Many writers have exposed the weaknesses in such attempts to assure quality (Barnett, 1992a; Duke, 1992; Trow, 1992). The issue now is what should be done. We turn to the conditions under which high quality learning will occur and then we ask to what extent various proposals about achieving quality are likely to lead to these conditions.

Under what conditions does high quality learning occur? The following statements may be truisms – they have been articulated in various ways by educators many times – but to give serious consideration to achieving high quality in higher education, they must be constantly reiterated.

High quality learning occurs when the learner is ready – cognitively, emotionally – to meet the demands of the learning task.

Readiness is an important concept in designing learning programmes. For instance, it is obviously pointless asking people to undertake tasks for which they do not have the skills. On the other hand, acquiring skills seems to be more effectively achieved if one wants the skill in order to complete a task at hand, so for the facilitator of learning there is a balancing act in structuring a programme: creating the need for the skill and then presenting the opportunity to learn it. Emotional readiness is less often considered than having skills or prerequisite knowledge in higher education but it, too, is important. Few teachers will have escaped the discomfort of watching a capable student collapse in an examination out of sheer anxiety, or a student who can write articulately freeze when called upon to speak. As learners in higher education classrooms become even more diverse, creating a climate which is conducive to high quality learning will become more challenging.

High quality learning occurs when the learner has a reason for learning. The better the reason, the better the learning.

Passing an examination is a reason for learning – often a pressing reason – and any discussion of assessment will reveal teachers' expectations (usually correct) that it motivates students. Hence the importance of designing assessment that encourages high quality student learning – not unthinking memorization of fact or regurgitation of lecture notes. But assessment should not be the only motivation for learning. Planning learning programmes so as to build on past experience and require learners to bring it to bear on new tasks, or giving learners the opportunity to initiate their own learning by setting themselves problems, or emphasizing applications and relevance of what may appear to be abstract or esoteric are among the strategies which will encourage learners to engage in high quality learning.

High quality learning occurs when the learner explicitly relates previous knowledge to the new.

One of the problems with curriculum planning in higher education is the specialist's assumption that learners need to acquire all the 'basics' before they can move on to the 'good stuff'. We do not wish to encourage this kind of thinking of knowledge in terms of hierarchies of content. It is worth quoting Gibbs (1992b) (who was building on Biggs' [1989] discussion of the key elements of good teaching) at some length on this point because it is so important:

> Without existing concepts, it is impossible to make sense of new concepts. It is vital that students' existing knowledge and experience are brought to bear in learning. The subject matter being learnt must also be

well structured and integrated. The structure of knowledge is more visible to, and more useful to, students where it is clearly displayed, where content is taught in integrated wholes rather than in small separate pieces, and where knowledge is required to be related to other knowledge rather than learned in isolation. Interdisciplinary approaches also contribute to a well-structured knowledge base. While conventional lectures may be able to convey the structure of a subject, they do not involve students in actively relating past and current knowledge into structures. (p.156)

We wish to encourage a recognition that even an 18-year-old has had many experiences and accumulated a great deal of knowledge (in the broadest possible use of the word) and it is the programme planner's and teacher's responsibility to help all learners recover relevant learning from their past and build upon it.

High quality learning occurs when the learner is active during the learning.

Logically no one can be entirely passive when learning, but there is a difference in the activity of a student transcribing dictation in a lecture theatre, learning the words or formulae and reproducing them and the student who is truly engaged in the learning process. People learn through doing; that is the foundation of problem-based learning programmes and there is sufficient evidence now to believe that they do, indeed, foster high quality learning (see, for instance, Boud, 1985a; Boud and Felletti, 1991). But even at more mundane levels, encouraging interaction between students in a lecture or designing assessment tasks which require different types of activity than library research or working sets of traditional problems can increase the purposeful and meaningful activity of learners.

High quality learning occurs when the environment offers adequate support for the learner.

Here we come to a condition which seems to be neglected, even ignored, in many of the discussions of enhancing quality. We have seen that in both the UK and Australia governments want to decrease even further the unit of resource. But libraries, laboratories and classrooms are obviously necessary parts of the environment and institutions – even relatively wealthy ones – are having trouble maintaining a very basic environment for learning.

One's first thoughts about support are usually for study skills programmes, counselling and the like. Then one thinks of support offered by teachers or programmes which may encourage flexibility through open learning or providing infrastructure for peer learning groups, etc. However, in addition the environment includes the climate of the society, the things people say and write about the institutions and their students. Students who constantly hear themselves condemned as illiterate or incapable – when they know they are among the highest achievers of their generation and are already working incredibly hard to succeed – are not getting much encouragement to continue with the effort. Nor are the staff of the institutions. And it is not only the academic staff who sometimes avoid telling a stranger at a party what they do for a living for fear of incurring another diatribe about ivory towers; support staff also bear this burden with the inevitable result of lowered morale and commitment.

Finally, within the institutions there is all too often a failure to recognize that the whole environment affects students' learning. Time wasted queuing for photocopiers or to do administrative tasks is more than an annoyance to a student who is travelling several hours a day and working part-time as well as carrying a full-time class load. Secretaries who seem to care about students' progress and who not only help them locate resources and make appointments but also encourage them to 'hang in there' at rough times of the year make a big difference to the environment. These may be mundane examples but they are part of what we mean by a total quality learning environment and which we emphasize throughout this book.

This articulation of the conditions necessary (but not sufficient) for high quality learning is consistent with other formulations by Biggs (1989), Gibbs (1992b) and by Kolb *et al.* (1991). Gibbs, building on Biggs, notes that of the four key elements of good teaching, none is concerned with classroom performance. That is, the key elements listed below could be present even if teacher and student(s) never entered a classroom:

- 'motivational context', emphasizing intrinsic motivation and need to know;
- 'learner activity', stressing doing but in planned activities, reflected upon and processed and related to abstract conceptions;
- 'interaction with others', which may be of various kinds but involves manipulation of ideas and negotiating meaning;
- 'a well-structured knowledge base' (see quote above).

(Just consider for a moment the limitations of some common attempts to evaluate quality of teaching through classroom visits or questionnaires about teachers' audibility or the legibility of overheads if these are accepted as the key elements of good teaching!)

In a textbook on organizational behaviour, Kolb *et al.* (1991, pp.58–9) address students directly and point out the ways in which formal education creates a false notion of what learning is and how it occurs: they describe how classroom learning is characteristically an activity divorced from the real world, an activity in which teachers have prime responsibility for the transmission of information which students acquire but do not apply. To try to counter this notion of what learning is and should be, they have explicitly crafted a text which 'is designed to create the learning environment that is most responsive to the unique needs of adult learners by addressing five characteristics of that environment' which they identify as:

- 'a psychological contract of reciprocity' which involves learners in both getting and giving as they receive new ideas and integrate and apply them;
- 'experience-based' which they suggest provides both background and motivation to learn;
- having 'personal application' in problem-solving within the learner's own context;
- 'individualized and self-directed' so as to be appropriate to the needs and learning styles of each learner;
- 'integrating learning and living' so as to learn both specifics of a particular subject matter and how to learn.

Having tested our formulation of the characteristics of and conditions for high quality learning against those of some respected others, we are prepared to use this formulation to help us achieve our purpose in writing this book – to encourage the development of a community of quality, a total quality learning environment. Where do we go from here? Not only must the community, or the stakeholders, share a conception of the overarching purpose of higher education and of the characteristics of high quality learning and agree that certain conditions are likely to foster high quality learning, the members of this community need to share some understanding of the research on student learning which underpins these conceptions. A summary of some of the key concepts from this research also provides a further test of the adequacy of our description of characteristics and conditions.

Learning about learning

John Biggs' (1989) inaugural lecture at the University of Hong Kong was titled 'Does Learning about Learning Help Teachers with Teaching? Psychology and the Tertiary Teacher'. The answer to the question was, and is, unequivocally 'yes'. But we would argue that it is not only teachers who need to learn about learning, it is all of the other stakeholders who need to understand at least the fundamentals of student learning if they are to make meaningful contributions to the improvement of higher education. Biggs wryly acknowledged the difficulty of a professor of education making an inaugural address in which one is expected to communicate the essence of one's specialism to new colleagues from a range of disciplines: when speaking of education to educators, all are experts. In fact, having experienced many years of it, almost everyone considers him/herself an expert on education. Thus, despite their sincere desire to help improve higher education, many stakeholders, including highly qualified academic staff, fail to appreciate that there is a vast body of knowledge about student learning which they have not accessed and which would challenge many of their treasured beliefs.

Biggs' lecture provides a most accessible introduction to current best thinking and practice in teaching and learning in higher education. The main theme is that to achieve the kind of learning we characterize as high quality in the previous section and which he names 'qualitative', in which learning involves 'meaning, understanding and a way of interpreting the world' ('deep learning' in the standard parlance), teaching must become an act of facilitation, not an act of transmission.

> Here the teacher interacts with the learner in line with the qualitative conception that learning involves the active construction of meaning by the student, and is not something that is imparted by the teacher. The teacher must know how to get students actively engaged in appropriate learning activities, but as Shuell (1986) says: 'what the student does is actually more important in determining what is learned than what the teacher does.' (p.23)

This conception of teaching as the facilitation of learning is contrasted with conceptions of teaching as the transmission of knowledge and of teaching as the efficient orchestration of teaching skills. Samuelowicz and Bain (1992) have recently reported research on conceptions of teaching held by academic teachers and note that only at postgraduate level do teachers in their project describe handing over responsibility and control to students, a conception of supporting student learning rather than of imposing on the students something which is still essentially the teacher's insight.

Two of the three conceptions of teaching – as the transmission of knowledge (usually in the limited sense of knowledge as information) and as the efficient orchestration of teaching skills (usually in the limited sense of teaching as presentation in the classroom) – seem to predominate in the various recommendations for the improvement of learning in higher education. For example, if teaching is primarily the transmission of knowledge, the mode of teaching is the didactic lecture and, if the lecturer knows the subject well and communicates it adequately, the students should learn. If they do not, it is their own fault. They may lack preparation; solution: fix the schools. They may lack ability; solution: raise the entry standards. They may lack motivation; solution: let them fail. Another logical approach to improving quality if the prevailing conception of teaching is the transmission of knowledge is to focus on the approval processes for new courses, which characteristically emphasize the completeness of coverage and currency of what is to be taught and whether there is a logical sequence of the content.

On the other hand, if teaching is conceived as the efficient orchestration of teaching skills, teachers work to adapt their teaching methods to different student needs and to different content goals. They are managers of teaching and if the students do not learn, the teachers need to be taught to manage teaching better. The solution: staff development programmes focused on teaching methods and emphasizing ever more sophisticated paraphernalia from projectors to computers.

These approaches to improving quality of learning in higher education may yield disappointing results. Staff development programmes of the type that focus on improving presentation skills, or on more sophisticated enhancement of teaching methods, or attempts to make course approval processes more rigorous are not necessarily bad moves; they are just not enough because they are based on conceptions of teaching which are inadequate to attaining the overarching purpose of all higher education: fostering higher order intellectual capacities.

Biggs discusses such approaches to improving learning and calls the first type, based on teaching as transmission, 'additive'. The additive approach looks for a single correctable factor which will lead to more desirable learning outcomes. In contrast, an interactive approach to improving learning 'assumes that as it is the students who construct knowledge, it is how they approach the task that will determine the quality of the outcome' (p.28). Think again of Barnett's reminder that it is the students, not the administrators or even the teachers, who achieve the aims of higher education (see Barnett, 1992a, Chapter 2; or Chapter 1 of this book). If teachers understand that learning outcomes are affected by factors prior to the learning – 'presage factors' in Biggs' '3P' model of learning – they must take into account not only the obvious, like prior knowledge, but also what conceptions of learning students bring to their classrooms. In addition, the learning outcome – 'product' is Biggs' third 'P' – is affected by the second 'P': process. Process refers to the students' choice, often unconscious, of how to do the learning. Will they take a deep, surface or achieving approach to the task? (A deep approach is one that seeks to make meaning and achieve understanding – high quality learning. A surface approach usually relies on rote learning and the student focuses on the concrete and literal rather than on meaning and connections. An achieving approach focuses on grades and doing what is necessary to gain good results but is not characterized by intrinsic motivation to learn.)

This critical choice can be influenced by the teacher's choices, particularly of methods of assessment.

> Messages that convey to students, whatever our intentions, that the assessments we carry out are just machinery for deriving grades invite cynicism; they will jump the hoops, and in return they will get their qualification. Deep engagement in the task is not part of the bargain. (Biggs, 1989, p.28)

Biggs goes on to remind teachers of the importance of providing 'opportunities that allow misconceptions to be made explicit' (p.29). Students need to explore their existing frameworks, correct false notions, and make the connections to the material currently being studied.

The project detailed below was informed by the research and concepts on which we based our description of the characteristics of high quality learning and the conditions likely to foster it. The case study reveals both teachers' and students' conceptions of teaching and learning and outlines an intensive and contextualized interaction aimed at improving practice.

CASE STUDY

Learning about Learning: Teachers' and Students' Conceptions

Peter Taylor, Queensland University of Technology

A number of indicators of 'high quality learning' were identified in the discussion above, indicators that I endorse. What this case study seeks to explore is the relationship between the notion of quality, as encapsulated by these indicators, and some specific and general perceptions held by both lecturers and students of their respective roles.

This work was undertaken within the Queensland University of Technology (QUT) during 1992–3 and was financed by two internal teaching and learning grants. The work, titled the 'Teaching and Learning in Tertiary Education (T&LiTE) Project' (the development of the project is discussed in greater detail in Clarke and Taylor [1993]), was conducted by a team of lecturers and research assistants working within the faculty of education's school of learning and development. (The lecturers were A/Prof Gillian Boulton-Lewis, head of the school of L&D, A/Prof John Clarke, Dr Paul Burnett, Dr Sue Burroughs-Lange, Barry Dart and Dr Peter Taylor. The research assistants were Jo Brownlee, Dr Alison Dyne [1992 to early 1993] and Shauna Cottee [early 1993 to end 1993]). The author, as well as contributing to the conceptualization and development of the project, was responsible for co-ordination of that project during its first six months and for its subsequent evaluation.

Five qualities made the T&LiTE project particularly distinctive; it:

■ involved volunteer participants;
■ focused on their individual needs and contexts;
■ provided support at a level and intensity that was controlled by them;
■ was conceptualized and implemented in terms of a cognitive view of learning; and
■ sought to provide support at a metateaching rather than teaching strategy level to the participants (Biggs and Moore, 1992, p.456).

Thus, the T&LiTE project provided support which was external to and independent of that available through informal means such as peer, collegial or professional networks, or through formal academic support units such as QUT's academic staff development unit (ASDU). As such it responded to the often unmet demands of lecturers for support which directly addresses their concerns in the context of their own teaching practices. Twenty-one lecturers and some 1700 students were involved in the project.

The case study briefly introduces the procedures involved in the T&LiTE project and then moves to a more extensive consideration of some of the perceptions of teaching and learning held by lecturers and students. From the analysis of those perceptions a number of implications are drawn, relating to both the value of the approach adopted within the T&LiTE project to professional development, and to consideration of the issue of quality in terms of teaching and learning. This case study calls for those involved in attempts to enhance the quality of teaching and learning in tertiary education to be sceptical of attempts to objectify and/or quantify the concept of quality.

The elements of the T&LiTE project

The project was based on several assumptions, the central of which was that the quality of learning outcomes is largely dependent on the approach that the learner takes when learning (Biggs and Moore, 1992; Morgan, 1993; Ramsden, 1988). This in turn is dependent on the conceptions that the learner holds of learning, what he or she knows about his or her own learning, and the strategies that she or he chooses to use. Learning is also influenced by the context in which the learning takes place. That is, course and institutional expectations are important in determining the strategies that most learners will use and the levels of knowledge for which they will aim.

The intention was to utilize the knowledge and expertise of the project team to document the knowledge of and approaches to teaching/learning used by the participating lecturers; share their understanding of the process of learning with those lecturers; collaborate with them in a review of their teaching practices so as to enhance quality educational outcomes for their students; and disseminate the results of the project widely. In support of this, the project involved an assessment of student approaches to learning; identification of the knowledge of learning held by lecturers; and assessment of lecturers' beliefs about and approaches to student learning.

We expected a number of outcomes from the project, but those of most interest to this report are associated with the collaborating lecturers. With them we intended to promote an increased knowledge of processes of learning, together with an increased understanding of and ability to design approaches to teaching which promote use of 'deep learning' strategies by their students (Biggs and Moore, 1992). This outcome seems quite consistent with the achievement of high quality teaching and learning as discussed earlier in this chapter.

The project involved a number of interrelated steps following the initial invitations which were sent to the deans. The main steps were:

- An initial group discussion of the participating lecturers with the project coordinator to discuss the project and negotiate details of commitment, support and involvement.
- A questionnaire survey administered by the research assistants during normal class time of those lecturers and of their nominated student groups to gather data concerning lecturers' and students' approaches to and understanding of learning in a tertiary context.
- Individual semi-structured interviews were conducted with the collaborating lecturers to gather descriptive data concerning each lecturer's beliefs about and knowledge of learning and the approaches to teaching which they used to support student learning.
- The student survey data were summarized and shared with the lecturers. The sharing involved an individualized written report followed by an individual discussion of that report with their T&LiTE lecturer. Those discussions were used to clarify issues arising from the report and to identify issues that each lecturer wanted included in our planned interview schedule for the student interviews.
- Semi-structured interviews were conducted by the research assistants with students who were representative of different approaches to learning and members of the collaborating lecturers' classes.
- The student interview data were summarized and shared with the collaborating lecturers through both written reports and individual discussions with their T&LiTE lecturer.
- A series of workshops were planned to be held with the collaborating lecturers.

The original project has been extended through a follow-up evaluation which began in July 1993 and is continuing. That evaluation has involved the opportunity for lecturers to gain feedback from their students on their work during semester II, 1993, through a replication of the student questionnaire (in a modified and shortened form) and interview procedures.

The T&LiTE project's approach to change

The strategy adopted was consistent with the call to enhance the quality of teaching by providing student feedback to lecturers 'augmented by conversation with someone with expert knowledge on teaching and learning' (HEC, 1992c, p.39). The focus of our conversation with the lecturers was the information on their students' perspectives on the teaching and learning context that each had created. That information was elicited and shared in terms of a cognitive view of learning, which was strongly influenced by the '3P' model of learning elaborated by Biggs (1991) and Biggs and Moore (1992). Thus our approach to change was based on the assumption that through the provision of this information and the opportunity to discuss it within a broad cognitive framework on teaching and learning, we would help lecturers become more aware of their own perspective on teaching and learning and support their reflection on the value of that perspective in terms of both their students' perspectives and a cognitive view of learning. Through this process of reflection on that information and the options for their practices suggested by that information and its discussion, we believed that changes in lecturers' teaching practices would be facilitated.

This strategy of providing conceptually structured information drawn from the context of their practices can be seen as a positive response to Ramsden's (1993) statement that:

> If we are serious about improving university teaching, we must look to changing the way in which academic staff conceptualise the teaching of their subjects, and how they embody their understanding in their practice. (p.95)

We used both their written responses to the questionnaire and our semi-structured interviews to explore their beliefs concerning major elements of teaching, and more specifically their beliefs concerning learning and their role as a teacher. Thus we sought to help them articulate their beliefs before we shared any information from their students and without attempting to offer any 'alternative' or 'preferred' set of beliefs.

Those initial explorations were extended when we met with them to discuss the responses of their students to the questionnaire and to later semi-structured interviews. Reports on the perceptions expressed by their own students were provided to each lecturer. Within several weeks of receiving their report the 'paired' member of the T&LiTE project team individually discussed the report with each lecturer. The intention of this discussion was to assist with its interpretation but not to be directive in terms of responding to it. Again, we sought to avoid imposing 'solutions' although the fact that our interpretations were framed by a cognitive view of learning means that the conversation was conducted within a theoretical framework whose use we modelled and value we advocated.

In addressing teachers' beliefs, two issues need to be clarified. First, that 'most of a [lecturer's] professional knowledge can be regarded more accurately as belief' (Kagan, 1992, p.73). The term 'belief' is used here to refer to ideas, convictions or principles that are accepted as true without positive proof (Hanks, 1979). That is, they are a type of implicit or 'taken-for-granted' knowledge. Kagan's (1992) research suggests that much of what teachers know or believe about their role may be silent in their normal conversations, implicit only in their actions or public statements. This knowledge is therefore not readily re-presented as empirical research 'findings'.

Second, a lecturer's beliefs have a degree of internal congruence. For example, their beliefs about their role are related to their beliefs about students' perceptions of the learning environment. Kagan's (1992) discussion of empirical studies resulted in two generalizations about this congruence, namely that:

teachers' beliefs appear to be relatively stable and resistant to change ... [and] tend to be associated with a congruent style of teaching that is often evident across different classes and grade levels. (p.66)

The latter generalization has significance in terms of Ramsden's call to change lecturers' conceptions *and* practices. Kagan's work suggests that if we can change the former, then the latter may have also been addressed. This is one perspective in a 'chicken and egg' debate about the relationship of belief to practice. An alternative view was provided by Guskey (1986) who found that changing practices led to changes in beliefs. The important point is that, given the evidence for congruence between them, it may be both unnecessary and unproductive to generate linear formulations with *either* belief *or* practice being *the* starting point.

The discussion now moves to some specific outcomes of the project of direct relevance to the achievement of quality teaching and learning, outcomes which were identified through the analysis of data collected within it. It is very important to acknowledge that these data and their analysis were the outcome of the T&LiTE team's work, of which I was but one member.

Some outcomes from the work with lecturers

(This section is based on Taylor [1993] and this first-level analysis was carried out by Dr Sue Burroughs-Lange, Jo Brownlee and myself.) We analysed the transcripts of lecturers' responses to the initial semi-structured interviews using the NUDIST (non-numerical, unstructured, data, indexing, searching and theorising) software program as a vehicle for moving from descriptive outcomes towards grounded theory (Richards and Richards, 1991). At the level of content analysis a conceptual model with five interrelated elements was developed and grounded in the statements from all the lecturers. That model represented the lecturers' beliefs about the nature of learning; the elements of learning that they valued; their concept of their students; and personal and professional relationships which formed part of the teaching/learning context as each of these related to their concept of their role.

Consistent with the work of Kagan (1992), our analysis identified very few instances of contribution of a formal understanding of learning to their role as lecturer/teacher. Rather, these lecturers' concepts of their role represent what Ramsden (1993) refers to as informal theories, derived from lecturers' experiences as learners themselves rather than any formal theories of learning. Several made this point during their interviews.

It also indicated that these lecturers saw their role as primarily involving two responsibilities: the delivery of information and the design of motivational learning environments. The former can be seen as indicative of a transmission view of teaching, while the latter reflects an awareness of the need to gain and/or maintain the attention of those students to whom the information was being transmitted.

While these generalizations may provide important insights into the broad picture, they are not seen as particularly useful in terms of helping individual lecturers address their conceptions of their role as teacher. To do this a more interpretative analysis of individual transcripts was undertaken to identify the patterns of emphases within the interview transcripts of individual lecturers.

What emerged from this analysis were quite distinct patterns for each individual, suggesting quite different sets of beliefs and (informal) theories about teaching, presumably with equally different teaching practices, given the earlier discussion of Kagan's (1992) work. The individual patterns, taken as a whole, were distinctive in terms of both the breadth of the elements that contributed to the perception of teaching and the significance of particular elements within it. We will use the analysis of three lecturers to illustrate this.

In terms of these levels of significance, lecturer 'A' seemed to conceive a role concerned with the generation of an interactive and practical learning environment in which she acted as a model of the learning she sought to promote, using strategies which rely on student reflection and self-direction. In this role she drew on her own experiences as a significant source of knowledge, yet she was quite concerned *about her own* limitations in responding to the demands of the role. The following excerpts from the interview transcript give some sense of this.

> ...what I wanted to do with them [Master's class] was to sort of get them to think about things more. I sort of wanted to develop it with them...(lines 332–5)
> ...so I don't know how to do it [teach this particular topic] so I thought well we'll research it together and hopefully they'll get something out of it and I'll get something out of it definitely, as well. (lines 343–8)

These patterns suggest a conception of her role as primarily one of co-learner (she used the term 'joint learner' in the interview) with her students. This may be very appropriate in the context of postgraduate level teaching in a rapidly developing discipline area – that of parallel distributed processing within artificial intelligence.

Lecturer 'B' appeared to hold a strongly focused view of her role which emphasized the development of interactive learning environments in which she nurtured students to achieve predetermined ends involving both tactical and strategic knowledge. Important additional elements included a focus on practical learning environments and extending metacognitive responsibility to her students.

> The feedback that I am getting at the moment is very positive. They come in and they are all beaming smiles. And they, most of them are pretty good chatterboxes, and they are dying to tell you what they have done. (lines 165–70)
> I had individual interviews with each one of them. It took a heck of a long time (laughs).... It really was time consuming. But I think it is paying off now, because it gave them security.... If they thought, 'Well at least I have some objectives, I know why I am here', and it was like a spring board into what was very, for most of them, very unfamiliar situations and environments. (lines 366–79)

She appeared to hold a lecturer-centred yet nurturing theory of teaching. This may be very appropriate in the context of first-year undergraduate teaching in a faculty of health.

In contrast, lecturer 'C' appeared to hold a view of her role which is more complex in its focus. It seems that rather than focus on the nature of the learning environment, she was more interested in the metacognitive quality of that environment, with a related emphasis on reflection. Her attention to modelling, to the strategic aspects of knowing that she was seeking to promote, and her awareness and use of her own experiences as the model for her practices are significant elements of that focus. This also extended to the use of evaluation, where she sought to establish expectations for deep learning and to focus on student performance primarily in terms of diagnostic rather than summative judgements.

[It] is probably more about structuring...your lectures, is giving them a framework. If they go to do learning and they don't know where it fits in, or how it fits in, then they will get very frustrated. (lines 607–12)

We are giving them solutions to tutorial questions with suggested marking guides, and getting them to do peer review. I told them it is only voluntary, but I have really expressly said 'If you get somebody else to mark yours, you are getting constructive criticism from somebody else. I mean, if you mark your own, you are going to sit there and say "Oh yeah, I knew that, I would have put that in",...well rubbish! Why didn't you put it in?' (lines 1084–98)

In general, she appeared to hold a student-centred and facilitative theory of teaching. This may be very appropriate in the context of teaching an undergraduate subject within a business degree programme.

Implications from the initial analyses

The first and most fundamental point to make is that this discussion indicates the need to see teaching and its quality in context. That is, measures of teaching quality and its improvement need to be sensitive to a range of contextual factors, including the discipline being learnt and the degree of familiarity of the learners with that discipline. The message, consistent with the work of Samuelowicz and Bain (1992, p.109), is that these contexts call for *different*, not similar teaching. Thus the achievement of quality should be seen in terms of a range of different qualities. Whether those different qualities can or should be combined to yield a 'single score' for quality remains unanswered, if not problematic. (See Hativa and Raviv, 1993, for a recent discussion of procedures relevant to this.) The use of such scores would seem to be most important to stakeholders remote from the immediate context of teaching and learning. On the other hand, the evaluation of this project, as an approach to the enhancement of tertiary teaching, indicates that the complexity and comprehensiveness of feedback was of great value to the participating lecturers.

The perceptions that each lecturer holds of her or his role, together with related perceptions of learning and learners, further fragment the possibility of a tidy concept of quality. While we were able to generate a conceptual model of the perceptions collectively evidenced in the interview transcripts, it was clear that each lecturer emphasized quite distinct aspects of that framework. Thus, any attempt to improve teaching will be mediated by individual perceptions rather than a generalized model. This can be exemplified through drawing on data obtained in recent interviews with the three case study lecturers, conducted in August 1993 as part of the evaluation of the T&LiTE project.

We asked each lecturer to comment on how their approach to teaching had been influenced by their participation in the project. Their responses included:

Lecturer 'A':
...it helped me in the sense that [it] made me realize that there wasn't only just one way to hold a class, which is the way it is always approached here. You know, the traditional, sort of handouts and you talk and then you tute. But it was good in that I had a bit of feedback from [the project lecturer] originally and we then basically agreed that probably for the first two weeks that we did have some sort of formal lectures until students knew what they were doing ... you know, not just throw them in the deep end. (lines 24–31)

Lecturer 'B':
...I do have the feeling that [the results suggested] I'd done a reasonable job and that's actually given me the confidence to carry on with some of the strategies that I used this time last year. (lines 15–18)
I don't know whether I've changed [any teaching approaches] so much as I've sort of adapted them depending upon the level of student because, as I've said I've got Master's students now, so its a slightly different approach. I'm also looking at group contracts now rather than individual contracts. ... It's not building, it's more developing those strategies rather than changing things. (lines 43–8)

Lecturer 'C':
It's been influential to the extent that things that were highlighted as good teaching practices I tended to try and go back over and use a bit more. Anything that wasn't highlighted as a good teaching practice I've tried to play down where I can get rid of it. (lines 10–13)

Implications from the evaluation analysis

A number of implications emerge from these comments, four of which will be discussed here. First, while these lecturers saw the project's specific outcomes in very different ways, their changes primarily involved elaborations of what they were already doing. They received and considered student feedback in the context of their own beliefs and practices. That is, they improved *their own specific practices in specific ways*.

Second, the fact that we discussed them in terms of that context seems to have been valued by these lecturers and to have positively contributed to any improvements. Again these findings point to a need to address the particular rather than the general context of tertiary teaching if one seeks to identify 'quality' and/or promote improvement in practices. Earlier I indicated that we intended to run 'workshops' as forums for sharing our knowledge and understanding of learning and contexts for reflection on, and the redevelopment of, those practices. While we made several attempts to initiate these forums, the lecturers did not support them. A number of reasons were given, but the main message we received was that their 'issues' were so individual and contextualized that they preferred to work on those issues in a more personalized way.

Third, the capacity of the project team members to focus attention on areas for potential improvement seems to have been critical to the decisions made by each of the case study lecturers about what changes to attempt. Thus the opportunity to converse 'with someone with expert knowledge on teaching and learning' (HEC, 1992c, p.39) appears to have been crucial to these outcomes. Lecturer 'C' commented that 'It's [the project] been good, and it's been good having the interviews and just being able to talk about it [teaching]' (lines 126–7 of evaluation interview). This implication suggests that the project provided a context for a 'fruitful liaison' between informal and formal theories of learning and teaching (Ramsden, 1993, p.94).

Fourth, the project's procedures appear not to have fundamentally questioned the underlying beliefs held by these lecturers. Day (1993) suggested that reflection on one's own practices is, of itself, unlikely to challenge beliefs. To achieve that outcome, he argued, reflection must be accompanied by the challenge of alternative beliefs (or practices). In this instance we did not overtly seek to make such a challenge, relying on the information we shared concerning their students' perceptions as a basis for our discussions with them. On the surface it appears that this has proved an inadequate strategy, as the underlying beliefs appear unchanged.

However, an alternative interpretation is available. Each of the lecturers interviewed in our evaluation identified changes in their practices along with a greater willingness to seek and value student perceptions. This returns us to the 'chicken or egg' debate. The evidence suggests that there have been appreciable (and appreciated) changes in practices. If Guskey (1986) and Kagan (1992) are correct, then there have or will be corresponding changes in beliefs, even though these lecturers seem unaware of that, as Kagan also predicted. This interpretation can be seen as stronger evidence of a 'fruitful liaison' between formal and informal theories, through a weaving of elements of formal theory into an individual's informal theories. The result appears to be an enhancement of the latter without major dislocation of its fundamental structure. The question that remains is whether fundamental restructuring from, for example, a quantitative to a qualitative view of teaching (Biggs, 1991), can result from continued evolutionary weaving, or whether there must be a more disruptive revolution.

While more work needs to be done to resolve this question, this project's outcomes suggest that there is considerable scope for improvement in the quality of many tertiary teachers' practices without a necessary pre-condition of fundamental change in their underlying beliefs, as called for by Ramsden (1993), for example. That is, the context of those practices is sufficiently flexible to accommodate useful elaborations of existing or similar strategies. It seems appropriate to continue to work towards realizing this opportunity while seeking effective strategies to facilitate more fundamental changes in beliefs/practices.

Some outcomes from the work with students

While the T&LiTE project focused on lecturers, it also represents a large investment in the identification and analysis of students' beliefs and the influence of those beliefs and context on their approaches to learning. I will restrict myself to sharing some outcomes related to students' perspectives on learning and assessment. The value of paying attention to the learner's perspective has been discussed by a number of authors, including Säljö (1988), who argued that 'Access to *the learner's perspective* on the activities of teaching and learning is essential for understanding educational phenomena – and for improving education' (p.35). If we have some understanding of their perspective, then we are better placed to make sense of their engagement with and reactions to educational settings. This is because the learner's perspective is fundamental in determining their reactions to those phenomena and settings (Ramsden, 1988, p.24).

The second section of the questionnaire invited students to share some of their beliefs about learning. The invitation was expressed as:

> Please write about a page or so on your ideas about learning. In that, you may consider such things as a description of what you think learning is, how you think you acquired that belief, what you know about your own learning, how you actually go about learning, what factors you think influence your learning and how they influence it, and how you know that you have learned something.

The questionnaire then provided two blank pages for students to write their response. Responses were analysed in terms of the SOLO system of classification (Biggs and Collis, 1982) and the conceptions of learning discussed by Marton et al. (1992). It is the latter of these two analyses that is focused on here.

Marton et al. (1992) reported a longitudinal study into tertiary students' conceptions of learning in which they found that learning was discussed in six distinct ways:

(A) Increasing one's knowledge

(B) Memorizing and reproducing

(C) Applying

(D) Understanding

(E) Seeing something in a different way

(F) Changing as a person.

These conceptions are seen as hierarchically related, with each conception subsuming those that precede it. Thus a person whose statements on learning 'fit' an *understanding* conception could be expected to include statements indicative of one or more of the preceding conceptions, ie, *increasing one's knowledge,* and/or *memorizing and reproducing,* and/or *applying.* The discussion here will focus on the outcomes of our analysis and not the procedures we used.

Tables 4.1 and 4.2 show the relative proportions, for the 1992 sample of students, of responses classified as representing each conception of learning in the undergraduate and postgraduate groups respectively.

Table 4.1: *Proportion of undergraduate students expressing each conception of learning*

	Conception of learning						
	A	*B*	*C*	*D*	*E*	*F*	*Total*
Number of responses	160	156	137	321	47	20	841
% for each	19.0	18.5	16.3	38.1	5.6	2.4	

In terms of the actual proportions of responses coded as representing each conception of learning shown in Table 4.1, a number of general comments can be made. The majority of undergraduate respondents saw learning as the pursuit of something less complex than understanding. That is, the majority of the undergraduate students have an essentially quantitative view of knowledge and learning, as discussed in Biggs and Moore (1992, p. 20). For them learning is primarily seen as an accumulation of the knowledge of others, a view that may reflect the demands of many undergraduate university courses. The proportion of undergraduate students who, in contrast with this view, see learning as associated with changing one's world view or oneself is quite small.

A comparison of undergraduate (Table 4.1) and postgraduate (Table 4.2) samples from 1992 suggests that students in the postgraduate sample, while including representatives holding each conception, tend to hold a more complex conception of learning than those in the undergraduate sample, although its small size suggests caution is needed in extrapolating here. What is most obvious is the much higher proportion of students whose responses were coded as seeing learning as associated with changing one's world view (18.6 per cent) or oneself (11.6 per cent).

Table 4.2: *Whole sample of 1992 postgraduate (coursework) students*

	Conception of learning						
	A	B	C	D	E	F	Total
Number of responses	6	5	9	15	3	5	43
% for each	13.9	11.6	20.9	34.9	7.0	11.6	

Interestingly, an analysis of proportions of students expressing each conception in different years of their degree programmes suggests that there is relatively little difference in the proportions of students holding each conception within different years in the one faculty. While this study was not longitudinal, this result invites a questioning of the assurance that 'students do become more sophisticated over time' as a result of exposure to the intellectual challenges of sustained tertiary study, as expressed by Morgan (1993, p.58). If this were true, then we would expect to see clear evidence of increasing proportions of higher order conceptions of learning associated with increasing years of tertiary study. While that may be true for some individuals, our data suggest that, in aggregate terms, such optimism may be unjustified.

These findings point to the need to question our assumptions about what students are trying to do in their courses of study, particularly in the context of an increasingly diverse student population. Morgan (1993) suggests that students are not likely to hold as sophisticated a conception of learning as their teachers (p. 55). This difference appears to be confirmed by our data. As a result they are unlikely to meet their teachers' expectations about purposes for their engagement in learning tasks. Earlier research (Doyle *et al.*, 1983) suggests that students are likely to pressure the teacher to lower her/his expectations, actively engaging in strategies to achieve this end. This pressure is reflected in the interview transcripts from the semi-structured interviews, as exemplified in the following extract:

> It's up to me to ask questions where I don't understand. There are a lot of people who, even if they do understand, they're too afraid to ask a question in front of a large lecture theatre because of the Australian mentality of not wanting to stand out. And also a lot of students, despite the fact that we're all here, we all know we're here to pass, but a lot of students don't want to seem too interested in a subject. It's not 'cool'. (student R6)

As a result teachers may adopt practices which unintentionally compromise the development of higher order cognitive skills and/or conceptions of learning.

Ramsden (1988) noted that 'a huge body of data has been collected' which shows that students in schools and colleges 'are unable to show that they *understand* what they have learned' (p. 14). Our finding that the majority of undergraduate students do not view learning as being associated with understanding raises the question as to whether the students to whom Ramsden referred were even *trying* to understand what they have learned. That is, we can interpret his observation as indicative of successful outcomes, seen from the students' perspective, rather than as a failing of teaching in the narrower sense of promoting students' understanding.

This interpretation reflects the assumption that an individual's conception of learning is a critical component of their world view. Marton (1981) pointed out that 'what we can see from one point of view may not have any representation from another point of view' (p. 184). It could be argued that if a student conceives of learning as 'memorization and reproduction', then this student may have little sense, or representation, of what it might mean to 'understand', either as an intention or as an outcome. This incompatibility of perspective is reflected in the interview transcripts also. When asked to comment on the relationship between teaching practices and their learning we found differences such as the following:

> To be honest, I'm just regurgitating for the exam. I just see the whole process as being [inaudible]. I know for myself there's a broader picture too, that I will retain a certain level of this material but the most basic thing from my point of view is that I pass the exam. (student M2)
>
> I'm trying to learn the whole thing rather than the bits I need to know. I'm doing this course to learn things, I don't have to do it. I'm just gaining knowledge and wanting to learn. (student RI)

Because each will have experienced it in terms of their intentions, which are clearly different, these two students are going to have experienced the same teaching in very different ways.

Consistent with the discussion by Biggs (1991) and Ramsden (1988), a focus for improving education that these findings suggest lies with the conceptions of learning held by students in addition to the more traditional focus on the subject matter being taught, that is metacognitive rather than cognitive knowledge. We would argue for approaches which orchestrate support for learning, drawing on strategies developed under the general rubric of both cognition and metacognition. However, we see that the conception of learning held by a learner will greatly influence her/his decisions to use such strategies, and predict failure and/or frustration for both teacher and learner where the necessary learning exceeds the individual learner's conception of learning.

The discussion of implications signals a need for lecturers to reject pressure to 'simplify' curricula and learning tasks where that pressure is motivated by a desire to please students. This is not to argue that complexity is a virtue. Rather, that having to engage with complex tasks is educationally sound practice if it is supported by complementary skill development and social processes, allowed to proceed over an extended period of time, and allows for alternative solutions and solution paths. This call for caution also applies to any interpretation of students' responses to 'official' evaluations of lecturer's work, particularly where that interpretation relies upon quantitative ratings of 'objective' items.

Project conclusions

Given these implications, what comparisons can be made between this approach to facilitating improvement in tertiary teaching and more traditional approaches?

While the participating lecturers identified a number of specific benefits of their participation in the T&LiTE project, a unifying theme that emerged from their comments was their valuing of its personalization which was reflected in many aspects of the project in addition to those alluded to above. For example, they valued the reports which we provided about *their own students' perceptions* of the teaching and learning context. Their comments also reflected a disappointment with more traditional interventions intended to provide 'solutions' in the form of 'better' teaching strategies. What their comments tell us is that they valued support which was focused on their practices rather than 'university teaching' or 'recommended practices'.

What our experience of conducting this project tells us is that such an approach is demanding in terms of the generation of the relevant data bases, their analysis and interpretation, the communication of our interpretations, and the discussion of those communications with collaborating lecturers. What remains unknown, in the context of decreasing per capita levels of resources, is whether those administrators and bureaucrats who seek 'quality assurance' about tertiary teaching are seeking improvement in quality or (just) reassurance.

Quality teaching and learning, then, are not to be pursued through a 'tidying' imperative, nor through a lecturer-only focus, but rather through constant and collaborative reflection upon the appropriateness of *particular* teaching and learning practices and the bases for such decisions. This conclusion stands in opposition to the suggestion that:

> It is undoubtedly the case that personal factors are vital in determining the quality of a student's education, a situation that puts some aspects of the learning environment beyond the reach of policy-makers at [national] and institutional level. (HEC, 1992c, p.44)

While it may be demanding to address specifics, I would want to caution against the implication that policy should address only non-personal factors, or that 'quality' is best understood (or measured) in terms of common 'performance indicators'. This caution is especially important in a climate of greater accountability, given that this climate heightens the attractiveness of all-purpose 'objective' formulae as *the* legitimate focus for improvement of tertiary teaching or learning, or the measurement of its quality.

Chapter 5

Encouraging Quality Learning

In the previous chapter we tried to articulate our understanding of what high quality learning is and the conditions under which it is most likely to occur. Taylor's case study described an attempt to use these ideas to influence both teachers and learners to develop conceptions of learning and adopt strategies which would lead to deep or qualitative learning. In this chapter we shift the emphasis to the contexts in which teachers operate and the many competing ideas and demands which often make it hard to do what sounds so obvious and simple on the face of things.

In his inaugural address in Hong Kong, Biggs (1989) sounded a warning. What he calls 'institutional context' is identified as a possible counter-force to the improvements which should result from an interactive approach. While an institution's rhetoric may be about high quality learning outcomes, its practices – requiring grades to be submitted on a particular day, allocation of teaching space, distribution of equipment funding, even course approval processes – may work against those outcomes. In addition, there are demands of industrial and professional bodies which also establish the 'social system' (Biggs cites Reid, 1987) of the institution. And back within the institution's walls are tradition and the expectations and norms of the teachers and students.

Limiting conceptions of teaching

Earlier we suggested that conceptions of teaching as the transmission of knowledge or as the efficient orchestration of teaching skills are inadequate if our goal is to promote high quality learning. If course approval procedures are based on these conceptions, it is quite possible that what purports to be a quality assurance mechanism may well result in promoting surface learning outcomes. Gibbs (1992b) provides a brief and accessible antidote to such limiting conceptions of teaching: a summary of research on student learning and the ways of encouraging deep learning through course design with a case study to illustrate appropriate course design changes.

He begins by reminding us of 'deeply disturbing' (p.151) research studies which provide evidence of students taking a surface approach to learning in all subject areas, in various types of higher education institutions, in later years as well as the first year; of students completing courses still holding common misconceptions about basic concepts of the disciplines they studied; and of students progressively abandoning deep approaches to learning in favour of surface approaches. And yet the standard examinations revealed none of these; these same students passed conventional exams and the performance indicators of numbers passing the course or numbers achieving a particular level of pass would have suggested quality had been achieved. Gibbs then summarizes the characteristics of courses which research has shown encourage students to take surface approaches to learning:

> The features of courses which are most likely to be found where students tend to take a surface approach are a heavy workload, relatively high class-contact hours, an excessive amount of course material, a lack of opportunity to pursue subjects in depth, a lack of choice over subjects and a lack of choice over the method of study, and a threatening and anxiety provoking assessment system. (p.154)

Gibbs and many others have called attention to the fact that typical responses to the challenges to higher education to do more with less are to adopt methods which are likely to foster surface approaches to learning with the inevitable result of lower quality learning.

Another consequence of course design which fosters surface approaches to learning is that students express 'very conservative views about innovations in teaching and great anxiety if alternatives to lecturing are suggested' (Gibbs, 1992b, p.155). That is, when students hold a conception of teaching as transmission of information rather than as facilitation and of learning as concerned with memorization rather than understanding, they are likely to reject attempts to encourage them to adopt deep learning strategies. There is another chicken and egg question here, related to those raised in Taylor's case study (see Chapter 4): do the students prefer conventional, teacher-centred teaching because they are surface learners, or are they surface learners because they have experienced almost exclusively conventional, teacher-centred teaching? Gibbs favours the latter explanation. Regardless of which came first, the performance indicator of student satisfaction may suggest quality where it is not.

Demands of diversity

Biggs' address to his colleagues concentrated on teachers learning about learning and, in particular, learning about undergraduate students' learning. So far this discussion has been based mostly on research on typical young (roughly 17–20-year-old) students who enter university directly from high school. There is an added complication in the system as it is developing now:

groups, by setting up self-help groups and tutorless groups, and by stressing group assessments as well as individual assessment. At a fairly mundane level, teachers might find it advantageous to provide for the greater use of, say, student-managed workbooks to support key lectures.

Teachers should make sure that learners are active during learning sessions, that they reflect upon their experience and relate this experience to theoretical models and explanations.

Learners should be made aware of the logic of active learning by exercises calculated to show the power of deep compared with surface learning. Students may be introduced to the 'action research' model of exploring instances of practice (see Chapter 6). Teachers may also encourage students to record their course experience and developing thinking in a portfolio which may be reviewed in meetings with others where the exchange of ideas and experiences arising from the portfolio occurs. Teachers should strive to vary the mode of class-based work so that no one mode tends to dominate.

Promoting responsibility in learning

It is important that students come to accept responsibility for their actions. To do so represents a recognition that we live in a social world and that our actions have consequences for other people. It is also vital that students come to feel in control of their learning and development and, to this end, students should be given opportunities for self-managed projects and self-constructed modules.

Teachers should create a teaching-learning environment that enables individuals to participate responsibly in the learning process.

They should allow learners to take responsibility for determining what, when and how they learn in some formal as well as informal settings, and for negotiating the completion and submission of work to deadlines. They should recognize that motivation for learning needs to shift from instrumental to intrinsic modes, and they may de-emphasize selective assessment and emphasize diagnostic assessment for feedback. In addition, they should foster opportunities for students to be sensitive to their responsibilities and duties, to recognize the needs of others and to listen to others.

Teachers should provide curricula that are flexible and enable learners to make meaningful choices in terms of subject content, programme routes, approaches to assessment and modes and duration of study.

They should provide more open and resource-based learning, including text-based workbooks. Teachers should enable students to access modular course menus and the financial/administrative procedures which accommodate discontinuity of study. In line with current modular course trends, teachers should allow students greater use of 'elective' modules from a cross-institutional menu.

Engaging with feelings and values as well as intellectual development

This has a particular connection with the value which we place on seeing people holistically.

Teachers should provide learning opportunities and encounters which involve the whole person, feelings as well as intellect.

There are a number of implications in practice: attempting to convey enthusiasm for the area of activity; conveying a sense of a joint endeavour in the pursuit of understanding; encouraging risk-taking and minimizing anxiety about errors; compiling a portfolio in which progress in learning is documented and reflected upon.

Fostering open, flexible, reflective and outcomes-based assessment

Teachers should provide a variety of assessments of students' learning, through self-, peer and teacher assessment where the criteria are made explicit following negotiation with course members.

They should encourage syndicate group members to provide formal and informal feedback to each other (inter- and intra-group). They should establish ground rules for avoiding 'group think' and mutual back-slapping (eg, a framework for critique of the assignment or project report). In course documentation teachers should emphasize what students will know, understand and be able to do at the end of a sequence of teaching. Teaching methods would be directed towards securing these learning outcomes (cf. Entwistle, 1992; Otter, 1992). In addition, the assessment strategies adopted should be congruent with clearly defined learning outcomes. Teachers may find it helpful if they adopt a wider range of approaches to assessment than is currently the case, including Records of Achievement which contain transcripts and materials from portfolios. To help clarify criteria, they may seek examples in the literature or in existing course documentation.

Evaluating teaching and learning

A prime condition for constantly improving teaching and learning is a planned and regular process of evaluation.

Teachers should engage in reflective professional practice.

Various tools for collecting evaluative data on teaching from multiple sources (including students and colleagues as well as oneself) are described in O'Neil and Pennington (1992) and Partington *et al.* (1993). The ethos of the 'reflective practitioner', described elsewhere in this book, is articulated by Schön (1983, 1987).

Teachers should design assessment tasks in ways to ensure that they are able to determine whether students have actually achieved the objectives of the subject. This is essential to meaningful evaluation of the effectiveness of teaching.

A new resource on assessment of learning outcomes is currently in preparation under the auspices of the Australian Committee for the Advancement of University Teaching (see Chapter 8). The project is based in the University of New South Wales' Professional Development Centre.

Teachers should foster a climate which values student involvement in the evaluation of teaching and the assessment of learning outcomes.

The NUS *Student Charter* (1992) sets out an agenda for the active involvement of students in evaluation not only about themselves as learners but also about the performance of their teachers. This is mirrored in the practical guide to student feedback written by Partington *et al* (1993). Such an involvement would mean, amongst other things, that institutions, course teams and individual tutors would need to develop student skills in giving feedback; set up more standard and systematic approaches to module and programme evaluation (some supported by information technology); and encourage staff to negotiate a mutually agreed two-way contract with students.

Establishing an environment (physical and social) to support the achievement of high quality student learning

Teachers and administrators must work together to fulfil this goal.

Teachers should do all in their power to provide not only a physical/ material environment which is supportive of learning and which is appropriate for the activities involved but also a social/psychological one.

On the one hand, this would mean that teachers struggle to ensure that adequate library and computing resources were provided by departments and institutions and also that speedy access to word-processing and photocopying resources would be a routine expectation. In conventional teaching programmes, better equipped teaching spaces and mass lecture rooms with a wider range of more sophisticated presentational equipment would be a common feature. On the other hand, in a 'new world order' of teaching, students would have ready access to more open learning resources and support. Teachers should help students access modular course menus and work to put in place financial/administrative procedures which accommodate discontinuity of study. In line with current modular course trends, institutions should allow students greater use of elective modules from a cross-institutional menu. Finally, the 'group maintenance' or social features of learning would figure prominently in the interaction among students and teachers to the extent that anxieties about work were minimized and enjoyment maximized. Institutions should provide academic and personal tutoring and more explicit educational guidance for informed choice in modular or programme systems as well as career counselling.

Ronald Barnett has been engaged in structuring a new programme of study at postgraduate level. In the following case study he reflects on the process of trying to put into practice principles similar to those we have outlined.

CASE STUDY

Challenging the Theory

Ronald Barnett, Institute of Education, University of London

Introduction

My aim in this case study is to examine the educational challenges in running a particular programme on offer in the Institute of Education, University of London. The course has recently been introduced, so the course team has not been able to carry out a full evaluation. The discussion that follows, accordingly, in no part attempts to offer solutions to educational problems. Instead, I use the case study as a means of identifying a range of problems common to many if not all programmes of higher education.

The course and its context

The course in question is an MA programme in *higher and professional education*. Almost all the participants are practitioners in the field, whether as lecturers or administrators. The majority are employed in institutions of higher education but a large number work in other domains, schools of nursing, professional bodies and as independent consultants. The age range is from mid-20s to mid-50s, clustering in the 30s, with women normally outnumbering men. While the programme can be taken on a full-time basis over one year, virtually every student studies on a part-time basis over a two- to four-year period.

At the Institute of Education, course teams have considerable autonomy in structuring a curriculum at MA level, albeit within the Institute's modular scheme. Students are required to accumulate 120 credit points, to acquire a minimum of 60 points in their main area of study provided that that study includes a 20-point report or a 40-point dissertation.

In our programme, we ask participants to take a 30-point module consisting of an overview of topics on (i) innovation and change, (ii) evaluation, (iii) ideas, and (iv) economics of higher education; a 20-point module on either (a) managing higher education or (b) improving teaching and learning in higher education; and a 20-point report or a 40-point dissertation (almost all students offer a 40-point dissertation). The remaining 30 points can be achieved by taking three from a range of six ten-credit point modules offered by the staff or can be amassed by taking modules on offer from across the Institute. The curriculum arrangements adopted by the course team require the participants to attend on one day a week, the session running from 4.00–7.30pm. Participants are, therefore, packing their MA programme onto what are usually demanding professional commitments. Many travel (for the UK) sizeable distances – often, well over 50 miles – and are reaching home late at night.

At the first session of the programme, each participant is given two brief questionnaires to complete. One is intended to give the course team insight into the students' expectations and approaches to learning. The majority of participants are, in the first place, looking to the course for professional development. Other motives are present, both at the outset and emerge as the course goes on, but there is a predominant intention to gain from the course some form of personal development that has direct professional relevance.

The course is currently attracting about 30 new participants each year. Given that some students are taking three to four years to complete, there are around 70 students registered on the programme at any one time.

I have been particularly associated with the course over the past three years, but two other members of staff have had a sizeable commitment to it, with others playing an important but lesser part. The course is offered by the Centre for Higher Education Studies whose staff contribute a diploma programme as well as being engaged on the full range of activities expected in the Institute of Education (writing books, conducting research programmes, producing consultancy reports, editing journals, giving conference papers and engaging in the further development of the host department and the Institute itself).

The current course builds on a former programme (MA in higher and further education) but has not yet seen a complete cohort pass through. Since we have no systematic data or evidence to hand, I shall plunge directly into the discussion proper by working through a range of issues common to higher education but drawing on the experience of this course. What follows is a personal account but I should much like to acknowledge the support and collaboration of colleagues associated with the programme (Professor Gareth Williams, Dr Roy Cox, Heather Fry, Robin Middlehurst, Allan Schofield, Dr Susan Weil and Maureen Woodhall).

Whose aims? Whose expectations?

In the UK we are seeing the emergence of a culture of student responsiveness on the part of institutions. Orchestrated by the government across public services as a whole, the policy has entered higher education and been reflected in the recent publication of a Department for Education booklet, *The Charter for Higher Education* (DfE, 1993). At the heart of this ideology is an attempt by the government to identify for the students-as-consumers their rights as to the character and quality of the services to be expected from their institution. To this, the academic community has responded by arguing that higher education is less a good which is consumed and more an interchange involving rights and responsibilities on both sides of the transaction. Some institutions have produced or are producing their own student charter along these lines (of which Liverpool John Moores University [1993] is a striking example).

This climate of student expectation is compounded where (i) there is a large proportion of mature students; (ii) programmes have some kind of explicit professional orientation; (iii) students are themselves in employment, and are looking for links between their professional experience and the course; and (iv) students' fees are met in part or in whole by their employer. On our MA, (i) and (ii) hold for every participant while (iii) is the case for most students and (iv) is the case for a sizeable minority. (It has to be admitted that this course offers a weak form of (ii) since unlike nursing, engineering or social work, for example, there is no professional body to which the course is accountable nor does it claim to develop professional skills to stated and demonstrable standards.)

The upshot is that the determination of course aims has to be problematic. *Whose* aims and interests are to be met? The academic community for the most part until recently has derived its legitimacy from its anchoring in disciplines and clusterings of intellectual problems, which together constitute intellectual fields (Becher, 1989). The student agenda may not be so securely rooted in matters of the intellect. If there is *any* disparity in the centre of gravity of the course team and of the students, to what degree should the course team attempt to respond to the students' agenda? After all, every cohort is different and will have a somewhat particular set of hopes for the course.

As we saw, the course team for this MA attempts to obtain an early indication of the students' approach to the course. But the question is one of principle. If the curriculum has been carefully designed with a certain structure and orientation, and if the staff have a certain view of their own professional responsibilities, to what degree is it proper to respond to the students' expectations? Or is a curriculum simply a pragmatic negotiation between the two sets of expectations? Or do we, as a matter of pedagogical *policy*, endorse the sociological point that a curriculum in any case will be largely constructed by the individual student, however it might be construed by his or her educators? This is a fundamental issue for higher education in the contemporary age.

Curriculum as process or outcome

This heading is doubly ambiguous. 'Curriculum as process' might mean a relatively *laissez-faire* stance on the part of the course team, enabling and indeed encouraging the students to see the curriculum as theirs. Here, personal meaning might be all-important, with little fixed in advance and the students being required to make their own choices over fundamental aspects of their learning experiences. Given that students register as a cohort and move through a course in numbers, there might also be much encouragement to persuade them to collaborate together, taking decisions collectively. This focus on personal meaning we might term a hermeneutic approach to curriculum.

However, 'curriculum as process' might have a quite different interpretation. Rather than allowing students to form and perhaps become trapped in their own meanings, a process approach to curriculum could attempt to do justice to the emancipatory potential in the notion of higher education, in particular putting critical thought at the centre of the curriculum. On a programme such as ours, concerned with higher and professional education, it would attempt to encourage critical attitudes to dominant concepts and practices in higher and professional education. Students would be encouraged to identify power structures, ideologies, the hidden agendas behind contemporary discourse and the dominant agendas *and* to recognize their own position in all this. *This* meaning approach is one founded on critique and would enable students, through their personal reflections, to undergo a self-transformatory process. (I come back to this notion below.)

Correspondingly, 'curriculum as outcome' is also ambiguous. It could mean a recognition that here are busy professional people with many demands on their time (including personal and family responsibilities) and that the course should be run so as to maximize the speed of their progress. The students normally – but not always – wish to gain their MA qualification in the quickest possible time. As is general in today's universities, the staff associated with this course are hard-pressed, with increasing expectations made of them. Accordingly, there is an inbuilt tendency on the part of both students and staff to wish to see that the learning is as efficient as possible. Increased use of course evaluation exercises, both at Institute and at national levels, also gives high marks to performance indicators and, on an MA course, perhaps the most telling indicator is the non-completion rate. 'Curriculum as outcome', accordingly, is here interpreted in terms of maximizing the output for the effort and resources available.

'Curriculum as outcome' might have further interpretations. It could also mean that an emphasis was being given to (i) assimilation and reproduction of ideas and information, so that the outcome is a knowledgeable graduate in command of a definite and predictable corpus of knowledge; or (ii) the acquisition of definite analytical skills, so that the graduates emerged with demonstrable skills perhaps of use to their employers; or (iii) the production by the students – especially through their 20,000-word dissertation – of a tangible outcome (which might also be of use in their professional situation). All these have in common a notion of education as product. On this conception, the student is a product, with added-value compared with his or her position on entry. It is the task of the admitting institution to add to this value.

Our stance on this course is to reflect in some way all these notions, the actual combination at any one time varying as a result of the interplay between the particular staff and the character of the cohort. Cohorts themselves take up different positions on the process-outcome axis, just as do staff.

One generalization, however, can be made but it gives rise to further questions. There is *some* sense among the course team that the curriculum has to be constructed, if only in part, by the students. Each student has to take some responsibility for his or her learning. At the time of writing, each student has to produce 40–45,000 words for the different assessed assignments and they have considerable latitude in choosing their topics. Further, given the range of age, experience and current occupations among the students, there is a recognition that their interests and approach to learning must lead to quite different learning experiences. The curriculum can never, in any circumstances, be entirely given. On a course such as this, a large element of construction by the students is evident.

Yet questions loom into view. To what degree is it proper explicitly to encourage students in their 30s and 40s to take responsibility for their learning? (The implication might be that they are not already doing so or are otherwise incapable of doing so.) Where students enter essentially with a sense of curriculum as outcome, how are they to be encouraged to develop a sense of curriculum as process? If the course is seen as a matter of personal appropriation of ideas and analytical techniques, how are more collaborative and critical attitudes towards learning to be fostered (within the constraints of a part-time programme)? Correspondingly, where students enjoy the process – and many say that it is therapeutic – might it not inject an unwelcome measure of direction and didacticism if more critical perspectives are to be imparted?

Or, quite differently, what responsibilities might staff have toward mature professional people to encourage them to structure their own learning so that it is efficient. Many are finding that their programme is slipping into a third and even a fourth year, not through any lack of commitment but through a reluctance to plan thoroughly and fulfil a personal timetable.

Theory and practice

Any programme designed either for those in professions or intended for those likely to find their way into a particular profession (and that means the majority of students in higher education) has to find an answer – or set of answers – to the theory/practice issue. That is to say that any such course has to bring theory and practice into *some* kind of relationship with each other. We could not be in the presence of a high quality course of professional education which kept the two realms separate from each other.

On our programme we recruit participants who are themselves professionals, with most holding appointments as lecturers or administrators in the field and who, as I mentioned, are usually looking to the course to assist them in being more effective in their professional practices. But precisely how might that aim be achieved? What kind of response would indicate a programme of quality? Is it a matter of supplying professional skills, analytical techniques, a new way of looking at professional problems, being able to bring disciplinary perspectives to bear on professional practice, or being able to deploy academic procedures and traditions in illuminating profession-related problems? All of these are different and all imply a different personal, even existential, realization of the relationship between intellectual and professional experiences.

The matter can be expressed as an issue of discourse. What is the primary discourse in which the course is to be conducted? Is it one of practical action, of practical reflection, of policy analysis, of disciplinary exploration or of wise and careful examination of issues? Is the outcome to be one of more informed action, of articulated experience, of practical recommendation, of empirical finding or of reasoned judgement?

It may be said that none of these matters is an issue of quality as such. An issue of quality, it may be felt, comes into play when decisions have already been made over the general orientation of the programme. Then we can assess the extent to which the course aims have been realized; whether, in other words, the course is fit for its declared purposes. This is an inadequate response. The logic is that a course can be whatever it might, or what might be determined for it; that there would be no limits. This line of thinking has to be rejected. In the present instance, for example, is it really to be suggested that a programme designed for professionals might not seek to bring reflection and action into a relationship with each other, that it would be legitimate for the programme to veer off entirely into a realm of discipline-saturated discourse? That, surely, would not be considered to be a proper path to take. Accordingly, there must be limits to what is proper as course aims. Quality judgements cannot just limit themselves to assessing the extent to which given aims have been met; the aims must come into the reckoning too.

Towards a learning community

As well as telling lecturers that they should think through their course aims and make them explicit to their students, the literature also reminds us that deep learning is likely to take place in environments which foster collaborative learning (Gibbs, 1992a). Students are a considerable resource. The injunction takes on a particular bite in the present course since the participants necessarily have significant relevant professional experience (normally at least three years' worth and often 10–15 years) and so there is bound up in any cohort a rich seam of varied experience. The notion of collaborative learning is, therefore, a definite part of the formal agenda for this course.

Collaborative learning can mean a variety of possibilities. First, it can mean students working together in groups on tasks set by tutors. These could be *ad hoc* groups attacking issues posed during a single session or could be more formalized syndicates working over an extended period. (We have not so far attempted the latter but make much use of the former.) Second, it can mean students engaging together on a specific problem such as a definite but hypothetical situation. If the problem is sufficiently complex, it will require the students undertaking some kind of inquiry or study (if only in the form of tackling a reading made available in advance): in this way, there is learning and it is collaborative. If there are opportunities for some kind of report, whether formal or not, to be made to the whole group, the teamworking element can be enhanced. Third, peer assessment might be employed. We have made a start in this direction with informal peer assessment of formative essays and may wish to move to a more formalized system. Fourth, a group assignment or project might form part of the formal assessments. We have not yet moved in this direction on this course although, in principle, if approached, I believe the course team would want to respond positively.

Quite separately, collaborative learning might have a more informal but no less important an interpretation. It could mean that opportunities are taken for students to learn about each other and to learn from each other's experiences and ideas. Here, the course team has chosen to encourage informal networking outside the timetabled sessions. Encouragement has taken various forms. The second of the two one-page questionnaires completed on the first day, in which participants set down a few points about themselves, is reproduced for all the participants. In this way, every participant has a directory about all the class members. This can act as a springboard for informal interaction. Encouragement has also taken the form of responding positively to requests or ideas from the students themselves. One group, for instance, organized a residential weekend for themselves. Another group would meet regularly before the timetabled sessions. In these instances, it was made clear that such extramural activities were the students', but tutors would assist on occasions, if asked. (For example, I was asked to give an additional lecture on a topic favoured in my writings, and was also invited to participate in the residential weekend.)

We are beginning to see signs in the literature of the notion of 'a learning community'. It promises much but is also vague. It carries the idea of students being fully engaged on their own learning, working collaboratively together and where hierarchical relationships between teachers and taught are reduced to a minimum. On this conception, all are motivated by an interest in learning as such. Learners recognize that interaction, testing of ideas, sharing of learning tasks, pooling of intellectual effort and mutual but supportive critique are not simply the best way forward; not simply the most efficient way of learning. On this conception, mutuality is understood to be the *only* way forward. If truth is in part an attribute of those ideas which are currently commanding some kind of consensus, if there are no private truths, then learning *has* to be a communal affair. The sooner we can get our students to recognize this characteristic of real inquiry, that truth is not given to be transmitted but is conversational in character (Fuller, 1989), the sooner will students begin to be properly educated. For then, they will educate themselves.

If something like this is implied by the 'learning community' and if we want to bring about that kind of atmosphere, ethos and self-understanding among our students, the educator is faced with considerable challenges and, indeed, professional issues.

There is, first, the task of winning over students to this way of thinking about their education. Students will often adopt relatively dependent approaches to their learning, expecting a highly structured programme which has been thought out in advance *for* them. Current moves to assess teaching are solidifying such attitudes. Further, where students are busy professional people attending, as here, a part-time course in addition to their many professional and family commitments, they want to feel that their learning is efficient and effective. Anything lacking in structure and direction is likely to be viewed with some suspicion.

There are, second, professional issues connected with the educator's responsibilities. What are the minima and what are the maxima of the educator's responsibilities? I do not believe that I have ever seen these simple questions addressed directly and yet they are of profound importance. How much should students have a right to feel that lecturers might do for them? How much can lecturers legitimately expect of their students in terms of the management of their own learning?

Those questions have to be put in the context of issues of student charters and of teaching appraisal and assessment, as well as of the research on learning quality. They also have to be filled out by distinguishing between different kinds of responsibility. Educators in higher education have a dual responsibility. Their first is to be on top of their subject. Preferably, they should be a practitioner of it in some first-hand sense. Not simply a keen digester of the latest books, journal articles or conference papers, they should themselves be active to some degree in the professional maelstrom of intellectual life in their own discipline. They can hardly bring about a learning community in their classes unless they have some immediate experience of forming and bouncing around their ideas in their own disciplinary sub-culture. Unless they are familiar with the knocks and bruises of academe – having a paper rejected, of having to respond to comments on their conference papers, of seeing critical comments on their books – how can they bring about a learning community which is more than a cosy culture and which has inbuilt critical standards?

The second responsibility on educators in higher education is both to be familiar with and to be responding in their teaching to some of the findings on student learning and curriculum over the past 20 years, but of even more importance to care and to think about higher education as such. What are they trying to do as educators? How might those aims be realized, given the students in front of them?

All of these views of 'teaching' cut across each other. Stimulating the students to take control of their own learning, to work collaboratively together is one set of tasks; being an authority – perhaps an international authority – in one's own discipline and sharing that understanding with one's students is an honourable calling, but is a different task. Being on top of the findings concerned with professional development, with curriculum design, teaching and learning, so as to provide brilliantly orchestrated timetabled sessions (of demonstrable worth to any assessor who drops by) is yet another set of tasks.

In what, then, does the authority and professionalism of the teacher in higher education lie? To say 'all of these' is a cop out – and we can muddy the waters still further.

On critical thought

No serious discussion of critical thinking can get off the ground without at least doffing one's hat to critical theory, whose major modern exponent is Jurgen Habermas. This is not the place for an extended discussion of Habermas' *oeuvre* in particular and still less critical theory in general. But some exposition there has to be. In any case, there are arriving in the literature attempts to link up Habermas' work with education (eg, Grundy, 1987; Young, 1989) although few attempts to interpret higher education with a Habermasian perspective (*The Idea of Higher Education* [Barnett, 1990] remains, I think, the only book-length attempt so far.)

Critical theory suggests that knowledge is permeated with deep-seated human interests (Habermas, 1978). Certain interests, notably those concerned with power and control, are tending to drive our knowledge efforts. In turn, these interests come to saturate our dominant social institutions. Since our knowledge efforts are being driven by limited interests, those interests also come to dominate how we understand those institutions, how we evaluate those institutions and how we drive them forward. If we are to do justice to liberal notions of autonomy and self-realization in our educational practices, it follows that education cannot be a purely personal and psychological approach. Education has to embrace a social and, indeed, societal dimension. Self-realization has to be an emancipatory project through which individuals come to appreciate the interest structure, ideologies and limited perspectives under which they may have worked or around which the professional setting for which they are destined is organized.

Against this background, we can distinguish critical thinking skills, critical thinking and critique. Critical thinking skills – if they exist – are skills which can be turned on to situations or cognitive experiences. They are the kind of thing employers have in mind when they say that they look for critical thinking skills in their employees. Taken-for-granted attitudes, beliefs and practices are to be placed under the spotlight of this searching instrument. This form of critical thinking has an instrumental character. Its value is to yield better operations and, ultimately, corporate results.

Critical thinking is the kind of thing that academics say that they prize. It is discipline-specific and refers to the forms of analysis and evaluation that are characteristic of the separate disciplines. Acquiring this form of thought is indicative that one has arrived, intellectually speaking. One knows how to come at the world and evaluate it, through the thinking of the physicist or the historian or whatever.

Both of these forms of critical thinking look to fulfil standards which are independent of the thinker. At least, the second disciplinary form betokens a change in the thinker, a cognitive transformation (Peters, 1966). In contrast, critique points to a change in persons, for through critique individuals come to see themselves, their beliefs and practices, differently.

Critique is the pedagogical application of critical theory. It says that this is the world that you are looking to be part of or are already part of (where, for example, students are themselves in work and studying part-time). The concepts that you deploy to frame your world, the professional practices, the fundamental assumptions about aims and purposes, may reflect certain and limited interests, probably of a strategic kind, intent on maintaining a set of institutional arrangements and on achieving certain kinds of effects. In an education in which critique had a major place, all these would be identified and would come under critical scrutiny. In the process, students would be reflecting on themselves. The educational process would be a reflexive journey. The students would come not just to challenge some of their ideas but would come to see through the beliefs and values which had constituted themselves. They would undergo an emancipatory process.

Such an educational process would be unsettling. It would be challenging the ways in which participants saw themselves. This would be particularly disturbing for those who were already occupying professional positions, often with many years of effective service behind them.

Meaning and critique

Much of the research into student learning over the past 20 years has suggested that learning approaches which foster deep learning – and, by implication, high quality learning – will be built around personal meaning (Marton et al., 1984; Ramsden, 1992). Students will get involved in their learning if they are involved in their learning! The tautology has point in reminding us that learning of any substance has to have a degree of personal meaning. Indeed, the label given to the learning approach receiving the highest marks is 'a meaning orientation'.

The problem, so far unrecognized by the 'meaning' and 'deep learning' advocates, is that pedagogical strategies oriented in this way may be a form of reproduction after all. What we may be doing is to foster the kind of learning that both academics and the state want. In this learning, students come to feel at home in the cognitive world presented to them or, indeed, which they construct for themselves. Ownership and meaning are the watchwords. But all of this may be to allow participants an undue measure of cognitive comfort. No boats will be rocked, personally, cognitively or professionally. Everyone is in favour of it.

What I am suggesting is that an education which is genuinely emancipatory in character may run against pretty well all of the nostrums we are receiving today, from educational researchers through state agencies charged with staff development and curriculum development to quality assessment methodologies.

Most students on our course complete the course and do well, and offer genuine thanks for their success. They know that, in many cases at least, their success is often the result of a long and hard joint effort, even though every one of their 40,000 words has been theirs. And yet, perhaps their world has not been sufficiently disturbed. For the most part, their practices and they as professional persons will not have changed greatly. Yes, they see themselves differently: they have greater confidence, they have perspectives by which they interpret professional life (and see it differently now) and they are more independent. So something has rubbed off. But the degree to which critical insight into their professional world has affected their view of themselves is bound to be limited for the extent to which critical insight is developed on the course is limited.

Perhaps we are doing as much as we can. We are doing as much as the participants want; but perhaps their view is limited. Student charters are an essentially conservative force and are not a vehicle for radical curriculum change.

The test of successfully emancipatory education would be whether participants were seized with a joint sense of transformatory possibilities in their professional lives and of themselves as change agents, but – to pick up the earlier points about truth-seeking and a learning community – the changes in question would have to be of a dialogic character rather than of a strategic character (cf. Freire and Shor, 1987). Having participants go off so that they were even more efficient managers or more efficient lecturers would not be the outcome of an emancipatory education.

Conclusion

Talk of improving quality in higher education is too easy. Educators who take the matter seriously are faced with genuine dilemmas which the contemporary literature does little to address. To summarize, just some of the tensions in front of educators running a course such as ours (only some of which have been addressed in this case study) are displayed in Figure 5.1.

The upshot of a list of tensions of this kind is both simple and problematic. It is simple in that there can be no final resolution, no definite uncontroversial settlement of what it means to improve quality in higher education. It is problematic in that as educators, we have to go on continually addressing and readdressing these issues. There can be no resting place. Every cohort will be different. Each year the journey, the puzzles, the debate and the negotiation begin anew.

A recommendation to ourselves (the course team) emerges out of these reflections. Having a reasonably clear idea of what we are trying to do on our course, coming close to a consensus among the course team, setting it all out explicitly in the documentation, having an introductory session and even sounding out every participant in one-to-one meetings do not constitute a sufficient effort to secure high quality. The range and number of expectations that we have begun to form, the expectations that we have of the participants both as individuals and – just as importantly – as a collectivity: these suggest that the course team should be spending time and effort in a more lengthy and deeper induction process, in which we explain what we are trying to do and engage the first-year students in collective dialogue at an early stage. This would be unsettling to many and we would run a risk of losing some at that early stage. Whether or not such an induction and early dialogue could be constructed so as to have only positive effects, I am not sure. I think, however, that at least we should try something of the sort.

Providing comprehensive documentation	Encouraging students to find things out for themselves
Students developing personal autonomy	Students working in groups
Time and space being given to processes of learning	Imparting of ideas, perspectives and analytical techniques
Meaning	Critique (critique may destroy 'meaning')
Detailed, constructive feedback from tutors	Peer feedback
Broad intellectual skills	Transferable personal skills
Applying concepts and techniques to one's professional situation	Developing a wider, even international perspective
Linking theory and practice to develop 'the reflective practitioner' (á la Schön, 1987)	Bringing academic discourse to bear on professional issues
Focusing on professional problems	Gaining a deep disciplinary-based perspective

Figure 5.1: *Dilemmas in promoting student learning of high quality*

Chapter conclusion

The goals of high quality adult learning, according to Knowles (1978) and Rogers (1983), should be to promote learning how to learn and the acceptance of an ethos of lifelong learning, namely:

■ intrinsic interest in learning for its own sake;
■ commitment to research, scholarship and critical enquiry;
■ development of study and information-processing skills;
■ willingness to experiment with new ideas and practices;
■ awareness of techniques for the effective management of tasks, time and people; and
■ recognition of own strengths and weaknesses, interests and needs and how to capitalize on these.

There is a difference in specificity but not an incompatibility with Barnett's (1992a) over-arching purpose of higher education and the characterization of high quality learning advanced in this book.

Biggs (1989) asked 'Does learning about learning help teachers with teaching?', answered that it does, and offered a primer on what has been learned about university students' learning. This book asks 'What is necessary for the system which comprises higher education to achieve its overarching goal of fostering high quality learning?' Part of the answer has been that those within the system – all the stakeholders – need at least a basic understanding of learning in order to work together to achieve the mutually desired quality outcome, what we are calling the overarching purpose of higher education. Without that understanding well-intentioned attempts to assure quality may very well be counter-productive. Hence, we have just offered our primer on high quality learning in higher education and how to facilitate it. Next we wish to elaborate on our concept of the community of quality: why it is vital to achieving quality learning, why it ought to be a congenial concept to those involved in higher education in particular and how we might encourage learning about learning within that community.

Chapter 6

Learning and Action Research

Achieving the conditions for high quality learning is a complex task not only for dedicated teachers but also for all of the stakeholders in the system which comprises higher education. In our review of government documents on quality we have seen many proposals. Despite the rhetoric emphasizing quality in learning and accepting that extramural stakeholders have roles to play, most of the proposals appear to assume that the responsibility for improving learning lies solely with the universities and primarily with the academic staff, thus ignoring the responsibilities of the other stakeholders. Middlehurst (1992) discusses the possibility that quality might become an 'organizing principle' for all aspects of an institution's activities. In surveying some examples of quality enhancement projects in universities, she notes that most focus on the domain of teaching (which is apparently what the extramural stakeholders would prefer), but that 'the way in which academic areas are related to quality elsewhere in the institution, or how different quality assurance or improvement mechanisms and procedures mesh together is not obvious' (p.34). Weil (1992), too, regrets that many RSA Capability projects remain at the margins of programmes or institutions. The case study in this chapter details a project which involves a number of groups from within one university, and the case study in the following chapter describes an even more ambitious approach. Nevertheless, to date most quality projects seem to have been somewhat limited in scope, with some notable exceptions (for examples, see Badley, 1992; Ellis, 1993b; *Higher Education*, 1993).

Learning context

Learning occurs in many contexts at once, some of them private and some of them shared, some of them under one's own control and some of them controlled by others. A student enters university and enrols in Philosophy I. Among the personal factors which affect the quality of her learning are whether she wants to learn to think 'like a philosopher' (she may first need to discover that philosophers have special ways of approaching questions). If she is to achieve that goal, the curriculum and the teachers will have to assist her to understand what it means to 'do philosophy'. If the tasks they set simply ask her to recount what great philosophers have written, she is less likely to learn to philosophize herself than if they challenge her to do it and give her constructive feedback. If the texts she needs are unavailable in the library, she will be less likely to succeed. If the student enrolment processes are inefficient and lead to the philosophy department suddenly having to cater for an extra hundred students, she may not succeed. If the government suddenly raises fees or changes the rules for financial aid to students, she may need to find part-time employment, and if the university has no employment service within its student services, she may have trouble keeping up with her studies as she seeks work. And so on.

If the systems of higher education in Britain, Australia and elsewhere are seriously to address issues of quality of learning, they will have to take into account the whole system – government, the rest of the education establishment, prospective employers in all sectors, professional bodies, the students, parents, the universities as organizations, all of their staff – not just the academics. All of the people in these categories are 'stakeholders' but much more importantly they are themselves part of the system. They contribute to its success and to its failure; some of them play relatively minor roles but they are part of the system. What we must be aiming toward is a learning environment that is, in its totality, high quality.

We cannot claim to have a programme in mind which will result in a total quality learning environment overnight or even within the foreseeable future. The vision of the elements of the system working together to achieve the overarching purpose of higher education – fostering higher order intellectual capabilities – is, at this time, only a vision, though in this book we sketch some possible strategies for institutions to adopt. However, there is a point in mission statements and articulating visions. They can serve to remind participants in the system of what is most important when they begin to bog down in details. We have been able to describe the characteristics of high quality learning and the conditions under which it is likely to occur. What would happen to some of the recommendations about improving the quality of higher education if their proponents asked the simple question: in what way does this recommendation ensure any or all of those necessary conditions for high quality learning? To answer the question, those making recommendations about higher education need to know something about learning and how high quality learning occurs. So they must become learners, too, and since some in the system know quite a bit about learning, they should be in a position to facilitate the learning not just of students but also of other stakeholders.

Recognizing that the stakeholders are themselves learners – most of them adult learners – and trying to apply what we know about individual learners helps us imagine ways of moving closer to our vision. We are going to restrict our discussion primarily to the institutions themselves for the time being. While they are not solely responsible for creating the quality learning environment, and while without adequate resources the institutions cannot possibly achieve quality, we must accept that they are the agents of higher education. Later we will see if any of the principles we discover may be applied on a wider scene or if there is some way of drawing other stakeholders in to share the learning.

Moving toward the vision

Keeping in mind the overarching purpose of higher education and the vision of the elements of the system working together to create the conditions necessary for high quality learning, we decided that it would probably help realize that vision if the participants in the system were to learn about learning. Since we know (or at least believe we know) the conditions necessary for high quality learning, and since we certainly desire high quality learning from all participants in the system, not just the students, we must try to produce those conditions in the programme we design for the purpose of helping participants learn about learning. We will seek to ensure that participants are ready – cognitively and emotionally – for the learning, that they have intrinsic as well as extrinsic motivation to learn, that the programme builds on their existing knowledge and experience, that it involves learning through doing, and that it offers adequate support to the learners.

A programme of facilitated action research aimed at improvement of student learning and the environment in which it occurs suggests itself. Here action research will be described and its appropriateness to realizing (or at least moving towards) our vision will be assessed. Then a case study describes such a programme in operation.

Action research

Action researchers study their own practices, their own understandings of their practices and the situations in which they practice. They do this to improve practice, not simply to describe it or to demonstrate the validity of some theory of practice. The effort to improve practice is part of the research itself. Lewin (1952) originally described action research in terms of planning, fact-finding and execution; now it is usually characterized (Carr and Kemmis, 1986) as a self-reflective spiral in which the practitioner/researcher goes through cycles of planning, acting, observing and reflecting, followed by replanning, further action, further observation and further reflection. The spiral is shown in Figure 6.1.

This process is consistent with the learning process favoured by adult learners outside of classroom settings which was described by Kolb *et al.*

(1991, p.59) as a 'four-stage cycle': (1) concrete experience is followed by (2) observation and reflection, which lead to (3) the formation of abstract concepts and generalizations, which lead to (4) hypotheses to be tested in future action, which in turn lead to new experiences. So we have a model for improving practice which is simultaneously going to provide an appropriate sequence for learning. The cycle is shown in Figure 6.2.

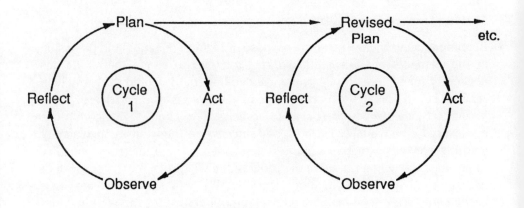

Figure 6.1 *Action research spiral (Carr and Kemmis, 1986)*

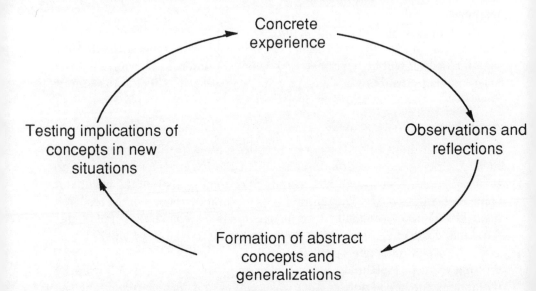

Figure 6.2 *Kolb's experiential learning cycle (Kolb et al., 1991)*

How are the conditions for high quality learning satisfied by facilitating a programme of action research? The nature of action research makes it impossible to force people to engage in it so we must assume that the participants in our programme are there by choice. The conditions of readiness and motivation are easily satisfied by the requirement for the participant to plan her own action research project enquiring into her own practice. She starts from where she is at the moment and the spiral builds from there. She works on something that she wants to improve. Pressures from within and outside her institution may also provide motivation, but the important pressure is intrinsic to the researcher who identifies a problem she wants to solve. Obviously, she is also building on her past experience and understanding and knowledge. In terms of readiness to engage in action research, it is the facilitator's role to help participants learn how to do it, but the skilled facilitator will, of course, use the experience as it evolves to help participants explore the process itself as well as the outcomes. So there are many layers of learning by doing involved in action research.

The support comes from the facilitator and other participants in the programme: although action research may be conducted in isolation if absolutely necessary, the ideal circumstances include the formation of a group of researchers helping each other understand what they observe. Even if the researcher does not have a support group of other researchers, the others involved in the activity she is studying and seeking to improve are her collaborators and help her to understand the activity and the outcomes of her interventions. Finally, in terms of engaging the learner in seeking out relations between new and old 'knowledge', that is the essence of action research (Carr and Kemmis, 1986, p.182):

> ...action research involves relating practices and understandings and situations to one another. It involves discovering *correspondences* and *non-correspondences* between *understandings and practices* (for example, by counterposing such categories as rhetoric and reality or theory and practice), between *practices and situations* (for example, by counterposing practices against the institutional permissions and constraints which shape them), and between *understandings and situations* (for example, by counterposing the educational values of practitioners and their self-interests as these are shaped by institutional organisational structures and rewards). [original emphasis]

The following case study demonstrates that it is possible consciously to foster an action learning network for the benefit of large groups, whole departments and the institution as a whole.

Facilitating Action Research

Ortrun Zuber-Skerritt, Griffith University (formerly University of Queensland)

At the University of Queensland, teaching development grants and secondments of teaching academics to the Tertiary Education Institute (the university's staff development group) have become increasingly popular and competitive. While these existing awards are designed to promote and reward teaching excellence of *individual academics*, the Department of Employment, Education and Training (DEET)-funded Developing Excellence in University Education (DEUE) grants in 1992 were intended to encourage *teaching teams* and *whole departments* to have a wider impact on the quality of teaching and learning in their own departments. The aim was to build a culture of quality and excellence, to strive for professionalism in university teaching and to build a 'learning organization'.

The area of building learning organizations is still largely unexplored and yet it is important in a time of rapid change. Senge's book, *The Fifth Discipline* (1990), has been a breakthrough in this field. The fifth discipline refers to systems thinking and building new types of organization which are decentralized, non-hierarchical and dedicated not only to the success of the organization but also to the well-being, growth and development of its members. Senge predicts: 'the organisations that will truly excel in the future will be the organisations that discover how to tap people's commitment and capacity to learn at all levels' (p.4).

A learning organization is a place where people are continually discovering how they create their reality, how they can change it and how they can create their future. The philosophy is that learning should be life-long and co-operative. It should be learning through discussion and dialogue. The original Greek meaning of *dialogos* means sharing of ideas and meaning within a group in order to discover insights which are not attainable individually.

The discipline of dialogue also involves learning about group processes, those that support and those that undermine learning. We are living in a time of rapid change generally, and in higher education in particular. In order to recognize and adapt to change and moreover to learn faster than the rate of change, we must develop a capacity to create new conditions, strategies and methods for solving new problems in the future.

The DEUE programme has been designed to provide a framework and to facilitate a process by which departmental teams can explore and share solutions to new problems, such as maintaining and improving the quality of learning and teaching in large classes with reduced resources. The purpose of this case study is to report on issues and activities of the programme and to present some conclusions and recommendations.

Providing information about DEUE

All information required by departments at the University of Queensland interested in participating in this project was provided in a booklet which explained the conditions under which creativity, change and innovation may occur; and how competences for excellence may be developed through action learning and action research.

This written information was complemented by an introductory session in which the main aims and objectives were explained in more detail, and members from the various departments had the opportunity to clarify any questions and concerns about the programme. This information session also introduced the 'Action Learning Program for Experienced Senior Staff' (both academic and administrative) and the 'Total Quality Management (TQM) Program', offered by the Tertiary Education Institute, and the difference between these three programmes.

Written information was also provided throughout the programme in the form of newspaper or newsletter articles, and at the end of the programme in relation to World Quality Day. Apart from invitation fliers, we sent out personal letters and produced a booklet with the programme and brief descriptions of all projects.

Establishing a framework for DEUE

A key workshop was designed to provide a stimulus, motivation and a theoretical framework for designing DEUE projects which would have an impact on student learning (deep approach) and teaching in the *whole* department. This key workshop was entitled 'Improving Student Learning through Excellence in Teaching and Course Design'. The workshop leader was Graham Gibbs, a visiting Fellow from Oxford Polytechnic who had conducted a similar, CNAA-funded action research project at national level in Britain. His recent book (Gibbs, 1992a) has been a popular resource for DEUE teams.

After this key workshop we had a follow-up workshop and individual and team consultancies prior to the submission of DEUE project proposals.

Procedures and criteria for selecting successful DEUE projects

Twenty-five DEUE proposals from 23 departments were submitted to the university's teaching and learning committee via the Tertiary Education Institute and assessed by a working party of the teaching and learning committee, who selected nine projects using clear criteria and proper procedures. These criteria were:

- identifying a major problem in relation to learning and teaching within the department;
- proposing a strategy likely to solve that problem;
- high probability of achieving the stated objectives;
- making a significant contribution to the improvement of learning and teaching within the department;

- involving a significant part of the staff teaching in the particular subject(s);
- department making an investment in staff time and money.

Unfortunately the DEET grant of A$150,000 was not large enough to fund all high quality projects worthy of funding. We would have needed over half a million dollars, but we could not have foreseen that the response to this proposed project of action research into student learning would be so overwhelming.

Similar procedures and criteria were used for assessing the final departmental reports and for prioritizing them in order to select the best project for the vice-chancellor's DEUE award. All panel members of the teaching and learning committee read each of the nine reports and assigned a grade of 1–7 using the following criteria:

- addressing a major problem in relation to learning and teaching within the department;
- developing innovative strategies to solve that problem;
- extent to which the stated objectives have been achieved;
- making a significant contribution to the improvement of learning and teaching within the department;
- demonstrated potential for wider application within the department and beyond (ripple effect);
- pay off in human and financial resources;
- extent to which the claims are supported by quality evidence;
- quality of presentation of report.

Providing support and shared resources

All winning departments formed an action learning community and met at least once a month at workshops scheduled into the DEUE programme.

In the first workshop, participants were introduced to the theory and methodology of action learning and action research. To begin with, they watched a video interview with Professor Reg Revans (1991b) and discussed the implications of his action learning principles for their departmental projects. Each team then formulated their focal question(s) and designed the first cycle in the action research spiral. Participants were provided with a folder containing all handouts and overhead transparencies, based on my books (Zuber-Skerritt, 1991, 1992a, 1992b) as reference material for use in this workshop and throughout the programme.

In the second workshop, the teams first gave their progress reports and the group shared their difficulties and problems. They asked each other fresh questions and suggested possible solutions to new problems. Each team formulated a long-term vision of the DEUE project and compared this vision (expressed as a picture, diagram or statement) with the stated objectives in the original proposal, with the actions to date and with what needed to be done next, by whom and when (action plans).

The third workshop introduced the Snyder model of evaluation and discussed this process of qualitative evaluation for action research. Bob Dick conducted this workshop, based on his work (Dick, 1991).

In addition, the Tertiary Education Institute offered a 'Quality Improvement Series' of three three-hour sessions on values and world views – led by Paul Chippendale – which was voluntary, but attended by most participants in the DEUE programme. The objectives of this series were to develop an understanding of the value system that underpins any quality programme and to develop strategies to build the appropriate value system. The following areas were discussed: the relationship between values and world views, between leadership style and values; quality management processes; and building and maintaining the culture for quality (see Chippendale and Collins, 1991).

In the final DEUE workshop we discussed the progress of the projects, any problems which might arise and the preparation for the written report and the oral presentation on World Quality Day. Participants' feedback at the end of the final workshop can be summarized as follows:

- The whole group unanimously agreed that the vice-chancellor's DEUE award of A$10,000 was unnecessary and counterproductive in an action research paradigm and in the spirit of an action learning community because of the groups' intrinsic motivation which was collaborative rather than competitive. The money would be better spent on a final residential workshop and a reward for *all* teams who had worked very hard and achieved high quality results. This residential weekend would be aimed at collective reflection, conclusions and future action plans.
- All teams wanted to continue their quality improvement programme.
- They considered the DEUE programme to be highly relevant to their teaching, learning and development needs.
- They regarded the DEUE projects as high quality, innovative, addressing important issues and as proper action research.
- They learned that many departments have similar problems and can learn from each other and that the action research process is valuable and appropriate for improving university learning, teaching and professional development.
- They also made suggestions for improvement of future DEUE programmes, eg. more funding and more time (one to two years), more workshops on evaluation, action learning and action research, and recognition by heads of departments of the need to adjust participants' workload and release from other duties.

World Quality Day

On 12 November 1992 – World Quality Day – we organized a big event, the DEUE symposium. On this day we joined organizations around the world in promoting quality. The inaugural World Quality Day at the University of Queensland celebrated, recognized and rewarded a number of new and exciting initiatives: the

University's action learning programme for senior academic and administrative staff and the departmental excellence in university education programme. The vice-chancellor opened the event and closed it with his 'Awards for Excellence in Teaching' of A$1,500 each to the three best teachers in 1992 (selected by the teaching and learning committee and supported by the university's alumni association) and the vice-chancellor's DEUE award of A$10,000 to the winning team, the department of anatomical sciences.

The university and wider community, the media and press were invited to witness this event and to be presented with brief (five-minute) reports from 14 teams outlining their aims and objectives, the outcomes and action plans for 1993 and beyond. All presentations were interesting, stimulating and of high quality. We produced a booklet for the audience with an introduction to the quality programmes, a brief description of action learning and action research, the day's scheduled programme, and abstracts of the team projects. We also published the three best-presented case studies (Ryan and Zuber-Skerritt, 1994).

Evaluation, results and outcomes

The DEUE project has been evaluated using continuous feedback from participants so that the programme design team could be immediately responsive to their emerging needs, as well as improving the DEUE programme for 1993 and beyond. In particular, the final evaluation questionnaire and the departmental reports assessed the qualitative (and quantitative) outcomes of the projects.

One coordinator typically summed up the benefits to him, his colleagues and the department:

> The grant is an incentive to write an application with a well-thought-out plan and rationale. It also leads to a required written report or paper, not just activities. It is more rewarding and exciting; it is accepted and valued in departments as a legitimate activity (like research), not just teaching improvement. DEUE can be integrated into the Department's goals and activity, rather than being an added-on individual staff development activity.
>
> Units like TEI have become too institutionalised and stale in their approach to staff development through seminars and workshops for individual volunteers. DEUE gets to the heart of the academic activities and integrates curriculum development and research. Colleagues who would not normally attend staff development workshops get involved in innovations and change almost automatically. DEUE gives me the opportunity to involve many colleagues in this innovation who would not otherwise be thinking along those lines.

Conclusions

The project proposal and design by departmental teams have been an effective way of improving learning, teaching and staff development. The DEUE programme fits the research application culture in academia and is accepted by academics as a legitimate activity.

Although the senior academics in this DEUE programme had high commitments to teaching, assessment and/or administration, they found the workshops worthwhile and useful for their own projects as well as for their understanding of the problems of other departments. The differences and similarities in these problems would not have become obvious to them if they had not participated in these workshops.

It was interesting to observe the ease with which participants used the new language of action learning and action research after the first workshop. At the end of the programme, many participants commented that they really understood the meaning of action learning and action research. They also mentioned that watching Reg Revans' video was 'a must' for any team before starting an action learning or action research project. People who had not met each other before formed an action learning community in the DEUE programme as a supportive environment of 'critical friends' and 'comrades in adversity' (Revans, 1991a).

My active involvement in these DEUE projects and in previous action research projects in higher education has led me to conclude that an action research approach to improving university learning, teaching and academic staff development is preferable to, and more effective than, other methods because of the participants' active involvement in the whole process.

Traditionally, external consultants, educational researchers or staff developers recommend sophisticated solutions to problems and changes in organization or curriculum design and development to encourage innovation and to enhance quality or effectiveness. However these changes, even if implemented, will not necessarily help and empower university teachers to solve their problems the *next* time(s).

By contrast, in action research academics participate in the problem analysis and definition; they collect data collaboratively and systematically (which constitutes the *research* component) and then take *action* on the basis of what the analysed data indicate; and they make their contribution to organizational learning. This is because they have the opportunity to develop their problem-solving skills, to make their hidden assumptions explicit and to examine their own process of goal setting, decision making and conflict management.

The difference between conventional quality improvement programmes in higher education and action research is that the former typically have a linear approach and assume substantial knowledge and clear, detailed goals before starting the programme. By contrast, the action research approach is cyclical and does not assume substantial knowledge before commencement. Goals and strategies are developed progressively and renegotiated at each cycle of the action research spiral. The participants are involved in all stages of the action research process, ie, in problem definition; strategic planning; selection of methods, strategies and techniques; implementation of the action plan; data collection and analysis; interpretation of results; and writing up the findings. Therefore, they are more likely to use the research results and implement the action plans than if the research and development (R&D) were done for them by external consultants or researchers, because they learn from the R&D in the first instance.

I am not suggesting that traditional research in higher education should cease to exist. It is appropriate when the aim is primarily to advance knowledge. However, if the primary aim is to improve practice, action research, if conducted properly, is more appropriate and effective.

Apart from my argument that action research is an effective approach to change and development in higher education, there are two main factors contributing to the success of the DEUE programme. The first is support from top management, ie, the vice-chancellor and the heads of departments participating in the programme. The second is professional support in regular workshops, which were conducive to the participants' team building, awareness of alternatives (eg, paradigms and methods, different value systems, etc.) and maintaining high motivation and energy to continuously improve their own professional practice and departmental excellence. The workshops also served the purpose of monitoring the progress of these departmental projects by both the DEUE programme teams and the Tertiary Education Institute. The evaluation, results and outcomes of this DEUE programme enable us to conclude that it was highly successful and may serve as a model to other universities.

Apart from the practical improvement of learning and teaching in the departments and the personal, group and organizational development and learning outcomes described by participants, the following *outcomes* provide *evidence* for the *success* of the DEUE programme:

- the written departmental reports submitted to the teaching and learning committee;
- the oral presentations of the DEUE teams on World Quality Day;
- the publication of the best papers selected by an international editorial board and edited by Ryan and Zuber-Skerritt (1994);
- the fact that the University of Queensland decided to continue the DEUE programme in 1993 from its own budget.

Recommendations

The successful practical and learning outcomes of the DEUE projects as documented in the reports of the participating departments and questionnaire feedback from individual participants suggest the following recommendations to universities and government funding agencies:

- encouragement of collaborative action learning and action research as an appropriate methodology for ongoing practical improvements of university learning, teaching, professional and organizational development;
- extension of the research application culture to research into teaching by practising university teachers, ie, the notion of 'teachers as researchers';
- a facilitation process by which funded project teams within a university (or across several institutions) meet regularly as an 'action learning community' to share resources and expertise, to ask fresh questions, to discuss problems, advise one another of solutions and alternatives and to monitor and review the progress of each project. This recommendation is particularly pertinent to the recently introduced National Teaching Development Grants of the Committee for the Advancement of University Teaching (CAUT);
- funds for longer-term projects, beyond one year;
- recognition and reward of excellence in teaching, not by means of a competitive prize, but by sharing a collective reward such as a weekend residential conference at the end of the programme to further the development of the projects and to reflect on the collaborative nature of action learning and action research.

Creating a total quality learning environment

For the purposes of working toward our vision of creating a total quality learning environment through helping the participants in it understand learning itself, action research seems to be the ideal vehicle. Regardless of the activity being studied, the practitioner/researcher can learn about learning through his/her own process of learning. Again the facilitator of the programme may aid this process of metacognition (of reflecting on thinking), but it is an integral part of the programme.

Even more importantly, action research is a process which can result in organizational learning. It has been frequently pointed out that if any organizations ought to be learning organizations – that is organizations capable of studying themselves and continuously developing themselves – universities ought to be. Since Argyris and Schön (1978) wrote about organizational learning, the term 'learning organization' has been bandied about rather lightly as if getting an organization 'to operate at a more self-conscious level' (Brown and Sommerlad, 1992) were a matter of will and staff development. Returning to *Organizational Learning: A theory of action perspective* (Argyris and Schön, 1978) is a daunting reminder of just how visionary is our ideal of a system working toward a common goal. Even the vision of an institution of higher education becoming capable of organizational learning seems close to a Holy Grail. Why is it so difficult to achieve?

Theory of Action

Argyris and Schön's 1978 analysis of many well-intentioned organizations failed to find one which was operating consistently as what they call a 'model O-II' organization and which we will refer to as a 'learning organization'; their later writings describe successful long-term interventions which assist both individuals and organizations to overcome the behaviours which inhibit organizational learning. A learning organization is one which is capable of detecting and correcting error, even when that correction requires changing the organization's norms, policies and/or objectives (double-loop learning). This ideal organization is also capable of 'deutero-learning' which is defined as learning how to learn. Such organizations are characterized by open communication and risk-taking; however, those characteristics are no guarantees of progress toward becoming a learning organization.

One of the difficulties is that the norms, policies and objectives may not be what the organization says they are; that is, the 'espoused theory', which is what the organization tells the world, may not be congruent with its 'theory-in-use'. For instance, an organization decentralizes its financial management, but annual budgeting remains in the control of a small group in the CEO's office; financial management is, in reality, still centralized. In addition, because most individuals adopt a theory-in-use which requires them to exercise unilateral control of situations, protect themselves and protect others from being hurt, they are not able to detect the underlying contradictions between espoused theory and theory-in-use, in either their own behaviour or that of the organization. The managers of the budget units in the decentralized system are unable to voice their frustration or discuss the difficulties they are having for fear of risking their own positions, but the longer they cover up problems, the worse the effects of the decentralization policies are going to be and the worse the managers are going to look.

Both the individuals and the organization wind up in a vicious circle, or 'primary inhibiting loop' (Argyris and Schön, 1978, p.85). Members of the organization interact according to their theories-in-use which reinforce and are reinforced by conditions for error. In the real world individuals can act as agents of organizational learning only by operating on information which is initially inaccessible or obscure (such as contradictions between espoused theory and theory-in-use). However, obscurity triggers the individuals' defensive and self-protective behaviours which, in turn, then reinforce the conditions for error.

Despite presenting a depressing series of case studies of organizations failing as learning systems, Argyris and Schön conclude their book with a statement of belief that individual members of organizations can learn to reflect on the ways their organizations function, can extend their capacity for seeing things from different perspectives and can develop more adequate ways of representing their organizations as learning systems, and that this individual learning will be 'complementary to the development of a more nearly [organizational] learning system' (p.318). In their analysis the individual is the key to organizational development:

> Just as individuals are the agents of organisational action, so they are the agents for organisational learning. Organisational learning occurs when individuals, acting from their images and maps, detect a match or mismatch of outcome to expectation which confirms or disconfirms organisational theory-in-use. In the case of disconfirmation, individuals move from error detection to error correction. Error correction takes the form of inquiry. The learning agents must discover the sources of error – that is, they must attribute error to strategies and assumptions in existing theory-in-use. They must invent new strategies, based on new assumptions, in order to correct error. They must produce those strategies. And they must evaluate and generalise the results of that new action. 'Error correction' is shorthand for a complex learning cycle.
>
> But in order for organisational learning to occur, learning agents' discoveries, inventions, and evaluations must be embedded in organisational memory. They must be encoded in the individual images and the shared maps of organisational theory-in-use from which members will subsequently act. If this encoding does not occur, individuals will have learned but the organisation will not have done so. (p.19)

Action science from theory of action and action research

The process through which the individual must proceed – discovery, invention, production, generalization – is very similar to the action research cycle. In fact, Argyris and Schön (1978, p.141) present a figure of wheels within wheels which represents their view that double-loop learning (see Figure 6.3) requires that the process must be applied to each step of the larger process; that is, the individual must discover ways to discover, invent ways to discover, produce them and learn and generalize, then discover how to invent, invent ways to invent, etc., etc. Wheels within wheels or spirals, does it matter? Probably not since both represent the process as continuous, never concluded. Argyris and Schön warn readers not to expect stable solutions. The 'organisational dialectic' (p.42) requires that situations give rise to inquiry and problem solving which in turn create new situations within which new inconsistencies and incongruities will come into play. If the process has resulted in organizational learning, the next round may not be quite so difficult as participants will know what to look for and how to look as they try to assess the factors that inhibit achievement of desired objectives.

Argyris' later writing (1982, 1990, 1991) offers more encouraging accounts of interventions as he increases his expertise in promoting organizational learning through exploration of the elements within the organization which

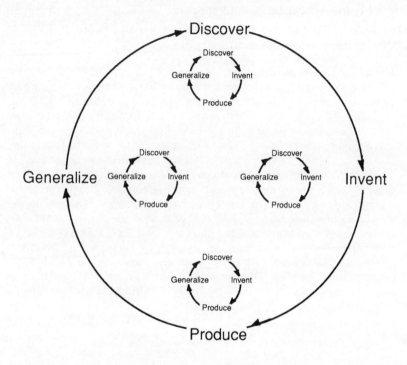

Figure 6.3 *Double-loop learning (Argyris and Schön, 1978)*

inhibit double-loop learning. However, anyone who wishes to pursue change through these methods must be prepared for it to take some time. Repeatedly Argyris and Schön refute the account of the relationship between theory and practice which is given by interpretative research – that 'transformations of consciousness are sufficient to produce transformations of social reality' (Carr and Kemmis, 1986, p.181). The key difference between interpretative research and action research is that action research, like the interventions of Argyris and Schön, requires that the participants seek to understand social reality, including their own role in creating it, but while developing this understanding is a necessary condition for change, it is not a sufficient condition. The participants in the system need to learn new ways of behaving and interacting, new ways of analysing their system in order to bring about change.

Action research, especially if the collaborators include other stakeholders, offers an opportunity to achieve learning which challenges the norms, policies and objectives of organizations and to help them learn how to learn about themselves. Carr and Kemmis (1986) emphasize that action research has, at least in its best manifestations, a ripple effect.

> As the action research process gets under way it becomes a *project* aiming at a transformation of individual and collective practices, individual and shared understandings, and the situations in which participants interact. From these particular projects, a *program* of reform emerges – each project embodies particular practices of collaborative self-reflection, employs particular understandings of the process of self-reflection..., and establishes a particular form of social situation for the purposes of self-reflection (what Habermas calls 'the organisation of enlightenment'). The establishment of a widening circle of self-reflective communities of action researchers in this way foreshadows and engenders a different form of social organisation.... (p.185)

To begin to move towards our vision of a community of people concerned with actively fostering high quality learning, we propose a strategy (like DEUE) of facilitating a group of action researchers addressing issues of importance to themselves; their projects lead gradually to a programme of reform. As they engage in their own learning, they learn about learning, so they are better able to answer the all-important questions: 'Will what I am doing help achieve the overarching purpose of higher education – fostering higher order intellectual capacities? Will it move us closer to a community of quality, a total quality learning environment?' They also learn about what promotes and what inhibits learning within an organization and are better able to become the agents of organizational learning. The researchers are encouraged to draw stakeholders from as many categories as possible into collaboration on their projects so the programme spreads as far and as rapidly as possible.

The 'particular form of social situation for the purposes of self-reflection' suggested by the interventions described by Argyris (1990) allows participants to understand their own theories-in-use and how they both shape and are shaped by the theories-in-use of their organizations. The goal should be not simply to fix something that is broken but to understand how it came to be broken and why it was not fixed earlier. Argyris and Schön (1989), or Argyris writing alone (1991), repeatedly ask why consultants and facilitators of organizational development do not ask their clients 'Why, if you knew there was an error, and at least some of you knew the solution, did it take so long for you to correct it? What conditions within the organisation made it impossible for you to act without this intervention?' Those are not simple questions to answer and require a great deal of individual and collective soul-searching based on observation and analysis of actual events and data.

Take the question asked impatiently by the Australian Higher Education Council (1992b, p.6): 'After all this time [looking back to the mid-1950s] the issue is perhaps not so much why are there now questions about transparent and public assurance of quality, but why are there still?' We are not going to be able to answer it but perhaps if we start to try to unpick some of the threads in the tapestry, we might discover some of the other questions we will need to ask. The government says (espoused theory) higher education is very important to the future of the country, but as it seeks to impose more control and monitor quality, etc., it would appear that government's theory-in-use is that higher education as it is now cannot help the country. Or perhaps the government is operating as a defensive organization and seeking to protect itself from blame by blaming higher education for economic woes. We need to test these attributions, not by simply asking influential stakeholders but by mapping their actions and analysing them and checking our conclusions again. We would need to repeat this process of trying to work out what lies behind various elements of policy and public statement. There is no doubt that there are many obscurities and inconsistencies but we cannot really be sure why.

Regardless of the reasons, one of the effects is to prompt defensive behaviour within the universities, such as denying that there is a problem with teaching, asserting that graduates are well-prepared, or blaming lack of resources. Our case studies reveal sincere attempts to improve the quality of teaching and learning, but most of them are problem-solving exercises; they do not ask, why is it difficult? Why has it not happened before? What can we do to change the organization so it won't be so hard in the future to bring about desirable change?

Inside the institutions the espoused theory is that teaching is very important. Almost everyone would say that the theory-in-use is that research is what really matters. Is that correct? What if we consider the amount of time devoted to teaching-related matters – writing new course proposals, documenting proposals to change courses, the various meetings to approve such proposals, class contact time, preparation to teach, marking, advising students. Is a proportionate amount of time spent on research-related activities? Why do people allocate their time as they do? What are their theories-in-use? They might tell us that regardless of the institution's reward systems, they cannot neglect their students, that their espoused theory – students are most important – is congruent with their theory-in-use. But perhaps those teachers fear failure as researchers – having grant applications turned down or papers rejected. Maybe at least some of them operate on a theory-in-use that is more like 'Research is very difficult and anyone can teach'. Maybe they blame the institution or the government and the pressure to teach more and more students with less and less assistance for their failure to fit in research. We certainly hear people saying such things but if the students really do come first, why do teachers not confront those responsible for promotions and demand different criteria emphasizing teaching? Perhaps aligning oneself with those interested in teaching and encouraging excellence in teaching is believed to be the best way of losing status in higher education. When such confrontations do take place, what happens? Usually the senior person becomes defensive and asserts that promotions on the basis of teaching excellence do happen, but that because of confidentiality names cannot be named. We could go on and on, just trying to imagine what really are the theories-in-use as regards the balance between teaching and research, but imagination and speculation are not what is needed. We need to make serious efforts at mapping the interactions within the institutions and trying to understand what makes them dysfunctional, despite the genuine excellence we also find within them.

People who want to take up this challenge will find many models on which to base their investigations in the literature of organizational development and educational administration. Our personal preference is for the 'action science' of Argyris and Schön and the insights they offer. In 'Participatory action research and action science compared' (1989), they align themselves with the action researchers but suggest that too often action researchers assume causal connections between their interventions and outcomes when other plausible alternative explanations are not tested; they also believe that many action research projects fail to take account of how defensive, self-protective ways of acting may distort the projects themselves as well as the interpretations of them.

Chapter 7

Organizational Change and TQM

While our personal preference is for a rigorous action research approach to improving the quality of teaching and learning (see previous chapter), recognizing that our preferences depend on our own learning styles and theories-in-use of which we ourselves may not be fully aware, we will canvass some other influential models of change to see what they may suggest and whether the strategy of promoting action research as a way towards achieving our vision is consistent with other models as well.

Lewin (1947) wrote of three stages in the process of change:

- unfreezing, for which there must be a strong felt need for change but which is accompanied by anxiety;
- moving, in which old ways of doing things are abandoned and new behaviours, attitudes and/or values are tested; and
- refreezing, in which the new ways are reinforced, internalized and institutionalized (or possibly rejected).

Although, as with almost any human endeavour, it is impossible to draw the boundaries between the stages very clearly, cases described by Argyris (1990, 1991) do seem to fall into this pattern. Those cases emphasize the length of time required for unfreezing and the strong resistance often put up by participants in the process who do not even recognize their own resistance strategies. Kolb *et al.* (1991, p.616) also warn that 'people do not easily change long-term behaviors', and cite the work of Dalton (1984) who described the sub-processes in which movement occurs in successful change programmes. The participants move away from generalized goals toward specific objectives, away from former social ties built around previous behaviour patterns toward new relationships which support the intended changes in behaviour and attitudes, away from self-doubt and lowered self-esteem toward greater self-esteem, and away from extrinsic motivation for the change toward intrinsic motivation. Nothing in the action research process could interfere with any of those sub-processes; on the contrary, a programme of collaborative action research should help firm up objectives, increase intrinsic motivation, build new relationships and increase self-esteem. Nor is there any difficulty in using the insights into the reasons that organizations do not learn which are provided by the various works of Argyris and Schön to help facilitate the change if the process is being conceptualized in this way.

As one reads the literature about managing change, one is struck by its congruence (see, for instance, Beckhard, 1990; Doyle and Ponder, 1977–8; Kolb and Frohman, 1970; Kolb et al., 1991; Nadler, 1987). Though various writers emphasize different aspects of the process – imperatives for change, reasons for resistance, different types of strategies for implementation, reasons for back-sliding, the role of the individual, the group or the organizational culture, structures, politics, et cetera ad infinitum – there really is not a lot of difference between the experts' views. The biggest difference seems to be between those who state that change should be a more or less controlled and orderly process (which could make potential change agents who have been through the mill before and had the process run away with them feel like failures), and those who admit it is often piecemeal and fragmented. Otherwise, various authors espouse more or less cynical and manipulative strategies for bringing about change, but the differences are often more in tone than in actual content.

There is almost always reference to the importance of assessing the climate for change, the readiness of the organization to engage in change. For instance, Kolb et al. (1991, p.615) offer the formula developed by David Gleicher of Arthur D. Little for determining readiness to change:

$$C=(abd)>x,$$

where C=change, a=dissatisfaction with the status quo, b=clear or understood desired state, d=practical first steps toward the desired state and x=the cost of changing. They (quoting Beckhard, 1990) explain:

> For change to be possible and for commitment to occur, there has to be enough dissatisfaction with the current state of affairs to mobilise energy toward change. There also has to be some fairly clear conception of what the state of affairs would be if and when the change were successful. Of course, a desired state needs to be consistent with the values and priorities of the client system. There also needs to be some client awareness of practical first steps or starting points toward the desired state.

Thinking about almost any university in 1993, one imagines an institution under great pressure from many stakholders in the system. Is that pressure sufficient to cause substantial dissatisfaction with the status quo? Frankly, we doubt it. Most of those within the walls of the institutions have a high degree of confidence in the work they do and a strong desire not to see higher education change very much at all.

Is there a clear or understood desired state to move toward? Not at all. The stakeholders, intramural and extramural, seem to agree on very little – they may not even agree on the overarching purpose we have put forward as a first step toward some agreement on goals.

Is there a practical, first step which we could take? We think so – facilitating action research projects aimed at improving the conditions for learning so as to increase the likelihood of high quality learning.

Since weight is attached to only one of the three variables to counterbalance the costs, there is not a lot to outweigh the costs of changing which are going to be considerable in terms of work and energy and the threat change poses to many deeply ingrained values, attitudes and behaviours. Using this tool could make any change agent looking at improving learning in higher education fold his/her tents and retreat as gracefully as possible.

On the other hand, action research projects do not need to meet all these requirements as they have a *raison d'être* in themselves. We hope they will have a ripple effect and lead to change in culture, etc., but even if they do not they are worth doing from the point of view of the researcher and his/her collaborators. Nevertheless, maybe some of the strategic advice in the literature on change will offer a way to overcome unwillingness if the cause is good enough and the agent foolhardy enough to persist.

Common advice is to identify resistance and receptivity so as to generate a 'critical mass'. The change agent asks:

Who is ready to oppose change generally?
Who is ready to oppose this change specifically?
Who is willing to let it happen?
Who is willing to help it happen?
Who is willing to make it happen?

Having worked out who is who (probably harder than it sounds if one believes Argyris and Schön about the prevalence of defensive cover-up behaviours and differences between espoused theories and theories-in-use), one is advised to take different approaches with different people to persuade them at least not to ruin everything. So 'rational adopters' can be engaged in the process of mutual problem solving through issue clarification, option identification and benefit analysis, while 'pragmatic sceptics' are attacked with analyses of costs and return on investment and appeals to enlightened self-interest. The 'stone-age obstructionists', on the other hand, must be 'overcome, removed, neutralised, bought off, worked around, or simply demolished'. Doyle and Ponder (1977–8) do not themselves offer this (somewhat offensive) advice; they, building on Sieber (1972), characterize these as the assumptions which lie beneath advice for overcoming resistance to change. They go on to show why it rarely works in the case of classroom teachers whose first and almost only criterion for deciding whether to implement innovation is 'Is it practical?', which seems to mean 'Is it practicable for me with my students in this school at this time?'

Nadler (1987) identifies three key phases in the management of change. First is shaping the political dynamics, which might include creating a senior planning group, designing special rewards for collaboration and increasing the visibility of the leader to demonstrate high level commitment to the change. Some of the techniques recommended for this phase are a bit less Draconian than those mentioned above, though many will, no doubt, reject them as manipulative. They include articulating a vision of the future while specifying what will not change, and using language systems, symbolic acts and small signals to help create identification with the change and a critical mass of support.

The second key phase is motivating constructive behaviour which includes creating a vision of the future, preparing people for uncertainty and defining the future state as made up of transitions. In this phase it is recommended that people be given plenty of information on the impacts and benefits of the change, that they be encouraged to participate in designing and implementing it, that there be ample formal and informal rewards for those who help and that sufficient time be allowed for people to disengage from the past. The third key phase is managing the transition and includes defining short, incremental transitions, maintaining the links between planning and transition management and increasing two-way communication. At this stage the design for the change must become as complete as possible, there must be adequate resources and back-up systems to cover the transition and constant feedback from those affected by the change.

From this advice, the reminders about keeping the change programme visible and rewarding the participants informally for their work are useful as we think of how our action research programme might break down resistance and help set up the organization for more sweeping change. An action research programme is clearly in keeping with the recommendations for not rushing things and for making transitions incrementally. Perhaps even more importantly, we are encouraged to continue to emphasize the overarching purpose of higher education and the vision of a community of stakeholders working to achieve it.

The strategies for change reviewed so far seem to be designed for use in organizations where leaders take control and lead from the front. Kolb *et al.* (1991, Chapter 20), in elaborating on a seven-stage process of planned change (see also Kolb and Frohman, 1970), speak of 'the manager' determining readiness for change, negotiating with entry point representatives, planning and executing action interventions and so on, and yet they also warn against imposed change and advise participation of those affected by the changes. There seem to be classic contradictions in the assumptions and values of the advice being offered. These contradictions are even more apparent in their discussion of the sources of power which they see as the main issue in 'gaining the influence necessary to implement the new program or method of operating' (p.594). Kolb *et al.* identify the primary sources of power and comment as follows:

1. The legitimately constituted authority of the system (eg the president says one should do this)
2. Expert power (eg the prestige of the consultant, or the compelling logic of a solution)
3. Coercive power
4. Trust-based power (the informal influence that flows from collaborative problem definition and solutions)
5. Common vision power, which taps into a common vision which many people share for the future

While in most change projects power from all four [sic] of these sources is brought to bear in implementation of the change, the power derived from collaborative problem definition is often especially critical to the success of those planned change efforts where the system's formal power structure and experts are seen as part of the problem to be solved.

One cannot help thinking that an organization which depends on notions of power, no matter what its source, is not likely to break free of the defensive and destructive behaviours which impede organizational learning.

Nor are these strategies or the images of organizations which they imply congenial to the kinds of places our experience tells us universities are, or which analysts have described. Universities have been described as anarchic organizations held together loosely by consensus. They have been characterized as lacking in integration, having virtually no horizontal integration and very little vertical (Clark, 1983). Another image is of a collection of warring fiefdoms, with the heads of academic disciplines acting as robber barons in the scramble for resources and recognition. Lockwood and Davies (1985, Chapter 2) explain the difficulties of managing universities as the result of their basic purposes, their activities and their history, noting that in a university different forms occupy the same body at once. A university is simultaneously an organization, a community and an institution; it is simultaneously bureaucratic and collegial. Regardless of which image one prefers to describe a university, the strength of universities is in the wealth of knowledge, talent and commitment within their walls which is all too rarely turned to the benefit of the institution itself. What kind of organization might mobilize those resources? What kind of change process would help achieve the vision of a community of quality?

The open organization model

Mink, speaking at a conference on total quality management in 1991, discussed the need to create new organisational paradigms for change. He spoke explicitly about resistance:

> In order to work through resistance we must be able to recognise its presence, its purpose, its origins, and the consequences of its operation in the life of the organisation. Managing resistance with intellectual strength, honesty, and integrity is one of the most essential functions of leadership in a time of upheaval. (Mink, 1991, p.194)

Mink places much responsibility on leaders within the organization for the task of identifying and naming resistance, but suggests the use of facilitators to assist with the dialogue about its causes and effects, especially the expected outcomes if resistance continues. To do this is to discuss the undiscussable in Schön's terms and it is impossible where fear predominates. Of course, the bind is that the fear not only inhibits discussion but also is itself undiscussable. Mink's solution is the new paradigm for organizations which he calls the 'open organization model':

> The organisation of the future will be based on the principle of adaptability rather than predictability. It will be an open organisation that considers process more important than structure, and free human interaction more effective than impersonal, chain of command hierarchy. It will be an intelligent, adaptable, learning organisation – one that can respond to shifts in a changing social environment. It will require that every individual who works in the organisation be receptive and willing to learn and to help others learn. It will require that every individual accept responsibility for the success of the organisation. (p.196)

In a paper presented at the Australian Institute of Tertiary Education Administrators 1993 conference, David Limerick (of the Graduate School of Management, Griffith University) described 'The shape of the new organisation: implications for universities'. Like Mink he is looking 'beyond the encapsulated corporate bureaucracy which characterises most Universities today'. He believes that in an age of unpredictable discontinuity, effectiveness depends on organizations being 'boundaryless'; they, in turn, require a culture of 'collaborative individualism'. The new/boundaryless organization is a concept congenial to collegial, non-hierarchical values traditionally associated with universities, says Limerick, and the flat structure, freedom from paternalistic control and emphasis on individual contributions (albeit within various networks) suit most staff. Limerick does not say so, and he was addressing mostly non-academic administrators, but his remarks often seem more representative of academic units and their culture and values than of the administrative support units where the majority of university staff are employed. We are not aware of any thorough attempt to observe, describe and analyse the two cultures existing side-by-side in most universities, but we believe the divide between academic and general (or administrative or support) staff is one of the most unfortunate complications to attempts to reform universities into learning organizations. Nevertheless, Limerick, Mink and others make a strong case for a reshaping of universities into open or boundaryless organizations with free and empowered staff who analyse their own problems and find and implement solutions on the spot without constant recourse to 'the top'.

Mink goes on to suggest that within the new paradigm organization, there is a new paradigm for change:

> All organisational learning and change are closely linked to the structures and complex interrelationships that define them. It is therefore critical that a mechanism for experimentation be in place so we can generate new paradigms or configurations around which we can reorganise. The new paradigm for change is the paradigm that:
> - optimises a high degree of energy exchange;
> - presents few constraints from structures, processes, policies and technology; and
> - is open and communicative both within itself and with other systems in its environment. This will require the organisation to have very open and permeable boundaries. (p.196)

This paradigm emphasizes change as a process rather than an event, a process in which learning and action 'intertwine'. Fundamental change, as opposed to incremental change, requires that both learning and acting are highly valued. This view of change once again seems to beg for an action research approach. Mink proposes five strategies (pp.195–6) to achieve organizational learning and transformation against which this approach may be tested and which may suggest refinements to the approach:

> - Tap into the deepest held values. Engage others as a group in the identification of cherished values. This can bind a group together for the pursuit of a common purpose.

Tapping into values occurs through the action research approach as individuals set their own agendas. Engaging others is part of the collaborative process of the research itself and of the support offered by other researchers who share their experiences and help each other understand them. Whether the goal (achieving a community of quality) and the overarching purpose of higher education (fostering higher order intellectual skills) are among the deepest held values of the members of the system is yet to be tested, but we believe they are.

> - Articulate a bold vision and communicate it repeatedly. An organisation's vision must inspire and bring forth the 'best selves' of

individuals in the organisation. Teaching ourselves to be steadfast to a common vision increases hope and nurtures creativity. Clarifying the purposes of a change effort also helps facilitate commitment.

Although the goals of particular projects may be limited and incremental, the larger vision may still be articulated and kept in view. If the organization as a whole does not immediately embrace the vision, there is still the ripple effect which we hope will build the critical mass. The nature of the goal is one to bring forth 'best selves', but there may be a difficulty in clarifying purposes in that the vision is a distant goal and it will take development and careful facilitation to establish clear shared purposes for the steps on the way.

■ Invite others to participate in the realisation of the vision. Establish participative processes for strategic planning and supportive procedures for implementation and evaluation. Maintain broad-based information flow, tapping resources and meeting needs. Most significant learning is acquired through doing. The optimum participation of others provides the opportunity for using one another as resources and results in the widest possible range of learnings.

Action research is participative by design. The facilitation can encourage researchers to involve other stakeholders (even those extramural) in the project and in its support and interpretation.

■ Become comfortable with and adept at managing resistance. One of the insights we have gained as leaders is that participation enhances ownership. While this is surely true, it does not fully answer our dilemma. Group analysts know full well that no amount of participation will protect a group from resistance. Resistance is always present. Only its intensity and its manifestations change. Resistance must be addressed or it will become more extreme.

To address this concern facilitators of a programme of action science could use Argyris' (1990, 1991) intervention strategies to help the researchers themselves understand the resistance they may encounter as they engage in their projects. Of course, they will be learning about themselves as well, the things which they relegate to being undiscussable and the contradictions in their own behaviours.

■ Do not hold individual people accountable for the system. Hold the entire system accountable. Everybody should be engaged as an experimenter and researcher in sharing ideas and in learning and problem solving.

Following this advice is, in fact, part of the vision which we wish to achieve. Drawing as many different people into the network of action researchers as possible and recruiting them from all categories of stakeholder is part of the strategy for helping them learn about learning and the ways to promote high quality learning.

Mink was addressing a conference on total quality management. We have been exploring the potential of a programme of facilitated action research to achieve change in the direction of fostering high quality learning through the shared efforts of various stakeholders in higher education. Do the TQM models have anything to add? Although the language of customer and product does not come easily to many in higher education, there are a growing number of universities adopting the TQM approach in response to government demands for a demonstrated commitment to quality (see Cornesky and McCool, 1992; Cornesky et al., 1990, 1991; Ellis, 1993; Higher Education, 1993). We include a case study later in this chapter.

Total quality management

The Deming (1986) approach to total quality management emphasizes the creation of a climate within the organization which makes work fun; the assumption is that human beings want to do their jobs well when they work in a quality-driven, customer-oriented environment, with full participation and mutual trust and respect among all employees. Because Deming estimates that managers control 85 per cent of the systems and workers control only 15 per cent, the responsibility for improvement is in the hands of the managers, but it will not be achieved without the help of the workers. One of the catch-cries of Deming-style TQM is 'Drive out fear', which is a goal of Mink's open organization model. In operational terms, this means abandoning targets and quotas, annual merit ratings and management-by-objectives performance appraisal. Cornesky and various associates (1990, 1991, 1992) have interpreted the Deming approach and those of Juran (1988), Crosby (1989) and Imai (1986) (also known as Kaizen approach) for application in higher education and offer case studies to illustrate.

The Deming approach is encapsulated in 14 points and in the identification of five diseases deadly to achieving quality. Again we will attempt to compare our vision and embryonic strategy for achieving it with this model, considering what experience reveals about higher education organizations.

The 14 points

1. Create a constancy of purpose. The organization needs a meaningful mission statement Creating constancy of purpose is one of our goals in trying to articulate the overarching purpose of higher education and to expand on that statement enough that stakeholders can ask themselves repeatedly, 'Is this recommendation, action, strategy or whatever likely to help achieve the conditions which will foster high quality learning?' Exactly how institutions incorporate the overarching purpose into their mission statements and then articulate specific goals to realize it will be up to them (see Allen, 1988), as retaining diversity in the system is very important as well as recognizing the one purpose which binds all stakeholders together.

2. Adopt the new philosophy. Everyone, starting at the top, must embrace a quality-based philosophy We have been developing the theme of a community of quality which includes all of the stakeholders in higher education. The nature of the enterprise is such that the sole responsibility for quality cannot be placed on the universities. However, it is hard to imagine a planned quality programme which would involve all stakeholders immediately. Indeed, where is the top of the whole system? On the other hand, institutions have implemented TQM programmes (see Badley, 1992; Cornesky and McCool, 1992; Cornesky *et al.*, 1990, 1991; *Higher Education*, 1993). The actual functioning of those programmes is not very different from engaging in action research and it is possible to involve extramural stakeholders in the programme whether you conceptualize it as action research or TQM. Starting at the top is not possible, nor is everyone going to share our perspective on what constitutes quality (see Characteristics and Conditions in Chapter 4), so at least on the wider front it seems unlikely that we will be able to meet this requirement completely. However, we can imagine moving toward it through the strategy we have proposed.

3. Cease dependency on inspection to achieve quality In the present climate with increasingly strident demands for accountability and the use of performance indicators to allocate resources, with industrial agreements requiring performance appraisal and at least one national body recommending national testing of the writing skills of university graduates (Smith, 1991), one fears that this is swimming against the tide. However, if we employ what we know about promoting high quality learning, especially in adults, and what we know about promoting double-loop learning, and if we do not lose sight of the vision, perhaps it is possible to gain some ground even against the tide. We may even be able to use our reports of quality assurance and achievement to improve understanding of what high quality learning really means and how to assess it. In other words, for all stakeholders, the stakes are too high to give up.

4. Stop doing business on the basis of price alone. Develop long-term relationships with suppliers who promote and support the organization At first thought, this point seems to be at some distance from the teaching-learning operations, but it should apply there as well as in support sections of the university in terms of equipment, resources for teaching and so on. It also may be interpreted to remind us that in the frantic quest for external sources of funding, we should not lose sight of the overarching purpose and the goals we are trying to achieve. The long-term relationships we need are with those who share the vision and understand what high quality learning is.

5. *Improve constantly*   Again there is consonance with the philosophy and methodology of action research programmes.

6. *Institute on-the-job training which includes orientation to the quality culture, which means all understand their role and its interaction with the whole*   Once again there is consonance with the vision of a community of quality and with the strategy of facilitated action research programmes. These are, indeed, on-the-job training and they can be implemented with both academic and general staff.

7. *Improve leadership. Administrators need qualities of vision and innovation*   Assuming administrators are involved in the programmes, this should be an outcome. We must consistently and energetically strive to draw the most senior people possible into our projects or at least ensure that the work is well-known – in detail – by them.

8. *Drive out fear. If work is fun, people take pride in it. Trust is the key*   With a programme which aims to move the organization toward the open organization model described by Mink (Mink, 1991; Mink, *et al.*, 1991) through the insights offered by Argyris and Schön (Argyris, 1982, 1990; Argyris and Schön, 1978), this point seems distant but at least in sight within the institutions. Trust among all the stakeholders, however, seems very unlikely in the foreseeable future, given the extreme statements being made publicly. The utopian dream is to have all agree on the one overarching purpose and the characteristics of high quality learning and then agree to try to achieve the conditions under which they are most likely to occur.

9. *Break down barriers between departments. A sense of belonging to the institution is vital. The programme requires participation by all*   Again this is the vision, but recognizing the divisions between stakeholders and the nature of the institutions themselves (little integration, warring fiefdoms, etc.), it is something to work toward while admitting that success will take some time. The strategies proposed are at least consistent with achieving that goal.

10. *Replace slogans, exhortations and targets with methods that work. There is no point in preaching quality if the equipment is broken*   We believe that the methods proposed can work, that they have been adequately tested and that they suit the culture of higher education institutions. This belief needs to be tested further, however.

11. Eliminate quotas and numerical goals and substitute leadership
Applied in higher education, this might mean that funding on student numbers alone should be abandoned. The idea behind the injunction is that with leadership the vision is constantly rearticulated and incongruent activities are abandoned.

12. Remove barriers that rob employees of their pride. There should be no MBO (management by objectives), no annual merit rating, but that does not mean no evaluation Some Australian universities have been trying desperately to avoid performance appraisal of this type despite industrial agreements which make it difficult to implement a programme of genuinely formative and developmental review of performance (see Abbott and Lonsdale, 1992). Hughes and Sohler (1992) describe the breakdown of a programme of developmental review for general staff in a university. Salary supplementation for academic staff, designed to assist in recruitment and retention of staff in areas where there is competition for their expertise is also a negative factor in trying to fulfil this requirement. On the other hand, pride and self-esteem come with learning and achievement and individuals should experience those outcomes as they engage in their projects.

13. Institute a vigorous programme of education and self-improvement
That is the intention of a facilitated programme of action research which includes stakeholders from as many categories as possible and which consciously tries to draw more and more people into the networks created as projects become programmes. Achieving the intention is the responsibility not just of those who conceive and facilitate the strategy but also of those who participate.

14. Involve everyone in the transformation to quality In addition to conscious attempts to expand networks and involve stakeholders in projects there is a need for communication about the programme and the vision which drives it – good old-fashioned sensitive public relations.

The five deadly diseases inimical to total quality improvement, according to Deming (1986), are:

1. Lack of constancy of purpose.
2. Evaluation on short-term results. It takes time to experiment with alternative strategies.
3. Evaluation of performance, merit rating or annual review. What is required is non-threatening, statistically significant, constructive performance review which encourages professional development, innovation and quality.
4. Mobility of top management. The best leaders abandon institutions which have high resistance to change and lack a quality orientation.
5. Running an institution on visible figures alone. Quality and innovation should be reflected in resource allocation.

ORGANIZATIONAL CHANGE AND TQM   131

Reviewing this list is cautionary, for we can see that these factors do exist in the system as a whole and within the institutions. It is going to require a paradigm shift to overcome them and we must recognize that our vision will confront and challenge deeply entrenched attitudes and behaviours.

The other key names in the galaxy of TQM gurus are Juran, Crosby and Imai (Kaizen). It is not necessary to recount each of these approaches in detail, but it is worth noting that Juran's is a more project-oriented approach but also more driven from the top than Deming and others; Clayton (1993) links the quality programme at Aston University with Juran. It is from Crosby that the notion of zero defects arises (prevention of error which is costly); this human resource-oriented, manager-as-facilitator model has been followed at Wolverhampton University (Doherty, 1993). The Kaizen approach emphasizes gradual and undramatic change and focuses on processes and systems rather than results and measurement of costs and benefits; effort is required to maintain the group processes.

While many American universities have introduced across-the-board TQM and some Australian and British universities have departments adopting the approach, initiatives like the one at South Bank University (UK), discussed in the case study which follows, have been unusual in Australia and the UK.

CASE STUDY

A University's TQM Initiative

Priscilla Chadwick, South Bank University

In the context surveyed in Chapter 2, the total quality management initiative at South Bank was launched in 1992. Recognizing the reality of increased student numbers (100 per cent over five years) and reduced funding per student, the need to improve efficiency and effectiveness was paramount: even a 1 per cent saving through improved quality in the way the organization was run would release around £700,000 towards improving the service to students. Three main reasons were cited for the TQM initiative:

- providing a 'quality service' is explicit in the institution's mission statement and reflects the fact that the vast majority of people in South Bank wish to do their job to the best of their abilities;
- the quality of South Bank's provision determines the university's success in attracting students and commercial contracts in an increasingly competitive market;
- the HEFCE quality assessments will take account of the quality of the student learning experience and this will affect future funding allocations: this experience is influenced both by academic programmes and the service students receive from all areas of the university.

The TQM initiative has two parallel strands in developing a quality culture: 'Quality in organization and service delivery' and 'Academic quality'. Both involve long-term processes towards quality improvement which encourage the initiative to be sustained at all levels across the university but allow immediate quality improvements to be made as they are identified. Both aim to help all staff maintain and improve their service to the students or other customers: the key determinants of quality are the attitudes and behaviour of staff.

Whether or not they are in direct contact with the students, the initiative encourages all staff to see themselves as part of a 'quality chain' of supplier/customer relationships that exist throughout the organization. When mistakes are made and the quality chain fails, the effects can be felt everywhere, absorbing expensive resources to rectify them. The person who operates at the interface between the university and its customer, be it the academic member of staff, the cleaner in the hall of residence, the telephonist who receives the students' 'phone calls or the counsellor in student services, will experience the ramification of any breakdown; but all staff, especially those who do not usually come in direct contact with students, need to realize the importance of their role in the chain.

> South Bank believes that the understanding and acceptance of this interdependence, through clear and persistent articulation of the concepts of TQ and the consistent application of principles of customer/supplier relationships, holds the key to the successful application of TQ. (Geddes, 1993b)

Three particular obstacles need to be overcome. First, staff sometimes have difficulty in accepting the notion of interdependence. University academics have tended to view support staff as 'second-class', often describing them negatively as 'non-academic'; similarly support staff often despair at the lack of administrative and managerial skill shown by academic researchers. Encouraging each side to recognize a shared responsibility for quality is vital.

Second, the isolationism inherent in a structure which allows academics to take sole responsibility for course design and delivery, only answerable to course or exam boards, can create a defensive or suspicious attitude to team teaching or class observation. The vital principle of academic freedom to explore one's subject without fear of interference or censure may provide a convenient smokescreen for those reluctant to allow scrutiny of teaching quality or the sharing of good practice.

Third, older academics have often seemed slow in coming to terms with the more competitive environment of modern universities and they resent the emphasis on attracting students or treating them as customers. Drop-out rates or overcrowded classrooms tend to be seen as a problem for 'management' rather than a challenge to rethink teaching methodologies or assessment strategies. One objective of the TQM initiative must be to break down unnecessary barriers and allow academic and support staff at whatever level to work together to enhance the quality of students' learning experience. TQM is a 'system of management that integrates a continuous process on improvement into all facets of all areas of an organisation' (Hibberd, 1993, p.477) .

Quality in organization and service delivery

There are no short cuts in the TQM process: it requires 'multiple transformation phases over a decade of time' (Torbert, 1992). The current TQM programme is now well underway at South Bank and may be considered in three phases.

Phase I

Phase I, begun in 1991, involved senior staff in examining the corporate process and culture of the institution, its constituent system, and engaging heads in devising draft statements of aims for their own units, schools or departments. Over the next few months other staff contributed to identifying the functions of each unit and the transformation process needed. From these transformation processes (sometimes dozens in each unit), departments drew up their own aims statements to describe their organization's intended performance and a list of draft quality standards and related benchmarks which could measure practice against the standards set.

Apart from formal departmental meetings, the participants were required to consult with a wide range of other colleagues in order to foster a sense of ownership of the quality standards and benchmarks. By April 1992, agreed aims statements, draft quality standards and benchmarks were published for every academic and support department across South Bank University. An example: 'Classes will have well prepared and appropriate handouts' – quality benchmark, 95 per cent.

Phase II

This involved the formulation of quality service agreements drawn up during 1992/3 by Customer/Supplier Working Groups (CSWGs) based on the draft standards and benchmarks. Such industrial/commercial terminology was not easily digestible to some and made it more difficult to interest staff and students, in spite of carefully explained definitions and clarifications. It was stressed that the quality standards must be realistic and achievable, with impossible standards avoided at all costs:

> It is absolutely essential that quality standards are developed by the staff who will work to them and not imposed by management. Quality cannot be imposed from above. (Geddes, 1993b, p.10)

At the same time, it was recognized that the original draft statements reflected the corporate aims and values of the university collectively arrived at earlier in the programme:

> it was hoped that in this way an effective balance between institutional imperatives and autonomous ownership of the TQ process at the school/ department level could be achieved (ibid).

TQM must involve both bottom-up and top-down leadership if real ownership and empowerment is to take place. Finally, it was stressed that quality standards needed continual review and updating, based on the monitoring of their practice and learning from the experience of other groups. There must be an agreed system of customer care to deal with complaints when quality standards were not met if the framework was to have validity or credibility. The finalized agreement would be disseminated widely among all interested parties.

Thirty-three different CSWGs were set up, including one for each of the 13 academic schools, one for each of the seven central departments which had substantial direct contact with students, one for each of the 11 support departments/units covering their relationship with the schools, one dealing with the relationships between each of the support departments, and one for the directorate. Membership of the groups involved representatives from a 'diagonal slice' of the hierarchical structure of the university, including academics, support staff and a cross-section of students. Each group was facilitated by a senior directorate colleague and provided with detailed workbooks outlining the TQM principles and specific guidelines on the process.

An interesting debate opened up about the leadership of these groups. If the head of the school/department was appointed as convenor, would this result in staff or students being less willing to contribute openly? On the other hand, it was felt that the heads themselves, being ultimately responsible for quality and managing the success of the TQM process, should take overall responsibility, though several appointed a senior member of their staff to implement the programme on their behalf.

The quality service agreements were due to come into operation in the academic year 1993/4, though some have needed more time. Data on 'customer care' were also available through course board reports, HMI or BTEC reports, external examiner or internal audit reports, student evaluations or the results of a student satisfaction questionnaire. Information might include, for example, data on the time taken to mark and return student assessments or the quality of constructive feedback provided. Issues were raised by staff about achieving certain performance standards if they were affected by factors beyond individuals' control, for example if teaching accommodation was unsatisfactory; some felt student 'empowerment' had its limitations; others questioned whether annual appraisal was sufficient sanction if staff did not meet specified targets. These and similar issues led into Phase III.

Phase III

In 1994, this stage involves setting up quality improvement teams to investigate ways in which the quality improvement goals of Phase II can be achieved and the plans implemented. Measurement of quality is not easy, but some attempt needs to be made to ascertain whether quality is improving, remaining the same or even declining. Measurement is also necessary to check if the performance standards set by areas of the university are realistic or need amendment, bearing in mind that these standards were set, in consultation with their customers, by the staff responsible for the delivery of these standards. The emphasis should be on facilitation rather than on directives, to empower all staff to 'own' their targets and achievements.

TQM is an on-going process of continuous improvement. Subsequent phases will be concerned with reviewing quality improvement achievements against plans, ensuring that any gains are held, evaluating and identifying successes, disseminating good practice and reviewing commitment and focus.

Within five years, it is hoped that the annual review of the quality service agreements will be firmly established as part of the annual strategic planning cycle. Linking TQM into the strategic planning process is essential in order to ensure that the university plans centre upon and constantly refer back to the delivery of a quality service to its student customers. In achieving this, South Bank can start to establish competitive advantage by 'achieving differentiation (of its courses) through quality of the learning experience, if a way can be found of advertising this to potential customers' (Clare, 1993). It is expected that up to ten significant quality improvement measures, for example in academic staff time saved by increased efficiency in validation procedures or in improved feedback from student course board representatives, will have been achieved at the cross-university level in response to common problems identified through the quality service agreements. Most importantly, there will have been a discernible change in the culture of the institution where all staff accept their personal responsibility for quality improvement as a natural part of their job.

Student satisfaction questionnaire

Alongside the work of the CSWGs, a comprehensive survey of student opinion was undertaken in the summer of 1993. A random 10 per cent sample of students was given a questionnaire, 83.9 per cent of whom responded, giving their views on a range of factors from teaching quality and personal tutoring to library and IT facilities. They were asked to indicate both their level of satisfaction and the degree of importance which they attached to any particular factor. (Similar surveys have been undertaken by the University of Central England in Birmingham.)

The results were decisive if not surprising. The quality of teaching was seen as overwhelmingly the most important issue, although library resources were not far behind. There were significantly higher levels of satisfaction among students whose course directors had provided them with quality course guides to assist them in planning and preparing for study, an initiative launched by the dean of educational development as part of the TQM programme in the autumn of 1993. The students' own identification of quality teaching and course organization as the highest 'customer' priorities leads us to consider in more detail the issue of teaching and learning as a central focus of a university committed to total quality.

Academic quality: issues in teaching and learning

The question of the quality of academic teaching is hardly new: Benjamin Franklin ridiculed the instruction offered at Harvard back in 1772. Academics have tended to focus primarily on their own research interests while permitting undergraduates or postgraduates to sit at their feet. Charismatic lecturers have their followers, but the extent to which teachers are conscious of the learning process in which their students engage is often minimal. There can be conflicting loyalties to subject disciplines, to the HE institution and its students, or to professional associations. Unlike research, where the recognition of peers is given for publications or through research grants, and where promotion prospects are favourable, good teaching is seldom acknowledged or rewarded (Cole, 1993). Subject knowledge, research capability and classroom practice are thought to be sufficient experience for effective teaching. 'Staff are expected to be competent in teaching but to strive for excellence in research' (Elton and Partington, 1991).

At the same time, a commitment to quality assurance for teaching is part of the central quality audit process now underway. Its lines of enquiry include teaching staff's competence and aptitude, the effectiveness of induction and staff development, and the action taken to maintain and enhance quality in teaching and learning. In what ways is South Bank University responding to this challenge?

Like many other universities, when the TQM initiative was launched early in 1992, South Bank had few effective policies in place for addressing 'quality assurance' in teaching. Staff development was under-resourced and, apart from a few poorly attended seminars, support for teaching tended to be remedial and confidential rather than proactive in focus. Individual staff in various schools had taken initiatives to develop more innovative teaching and learning strategies, but there was little coherence or expectation of exchanging ideas, so that good practice remained patchy and isolated. South Bank had missed out on the opportunity for 'Enterprise' funding and it showed.

Induction to the university was effective and appreciated by new staff, but limited to meeting senior members of staff and touring key areas of the facilities or buildings. An administrative memorandum from December 1972 stated that new teaching staff should be provided with mentors and given reduced teaching schedules in their first year; the reality in a number of schools was that new staff were given the classes others were reluctant to teach on the assumption that, if they survived their probationary year, they would have an easier time later on. Appraisal and staff development procedures were then under discussion, but staff representatives were apprehensive about sharing good classroom practice or recognizing the more developmental approaches to staff development beyond sabbatical requests. There was indeed much to do on teaching quality.

Some would claim that quality assurance in teaching has never been a problem; after all it is evident first in students' examination results verified by external examiners and, second, in the formal course validation and review procedures.

Questions however have been raised (cf. Ellis, 1993b, p.9) about the confidence of such arguments: external examiners, usually teachers themselves, are rarely willing to comment on the quality of colleagues' teaching and even in course documents the required sections on teaching and learning are often perfunctory, addressing pedagogical issues in routine terminology.

All of this pointed to the need for a radical and imaginative staff development programme as part of the TQM initiative. Indeed, as Gore (1993) suggests:

> Properly applied, we can expect TQM to impact the quality of teaching by encouraging a culture more open to change, teamwork, cross-functional co-operation and new technology. (p.356)

Of paramount importance was the effective induction and training of academics newly appointed to teaching. As the appraisal process began to identify staff development needs, there also needed to be clear procedures and resources for responding to individual requests. The quality of material produced for students needed review and the exciting developments in multi-media and hypercourseware had to be harnessed to enhance teaching and learning across the university.

Postgraduate Certificate in Higher Education (PGCHE)

More resources became available in 1992 through the Polytechnics and Colleges Funding Council (PCFC) to support academic staff development. As recruitment of staff well qualified in their own fields increased to meet the rise in student numbers, so the needs of these staff in the area of teaching skills became more apparent. The teaching environment of universities in the 1990s was radically different from a decade earlier: staff faced lecture rooms of 250+ students, seminars were now likely to have 70 rather than 25 students and one-to-one tutorials were a distant memory. A number of older staff in the university had attended a post-compulsory education training course in London in the 1970s, but its emphasis had tended to be more on further than higher education. For newly appointed staff coming straight from careers in industry, commerce, the legal profession or the health service, the task was daunting.

At the same time, the increasing interest in accreditation of prior learning, records of achievement and portfolio evidence encouraged staff at South Bank University to recognize that the valuable work done by new lecturers ought to be more formally accredited. The 'reflective practitioner' model (Schön, 1983, 1987) particularly relevant in teacher and health education should be just as appropriate for university teachers. A national framework for the Accreditation of Teachers in Higher Education was then being developed by the Standing Conference on Educational Development (SCED), now amalgamated with other university staff developers to form the Staff and Educational Development Association (SEDA). Various models of lecturer training had been adopted around the country (eg, Brighton, Oxford, Newcastle, Teesside). The demand for a formal qualification (rather than just a survival course in teaching skills) was increasingly being articulated by senior staff concerned with quality assurance and from new lecturers who wished to enhance their career prospects in a more competitive job market.

After extensive consultation, the university decided to offer a PGCHE course to all new staff appointed without teaching qualifications or at least two years' full-time experience in higher education, from September 1992. It would provide ten CATS points at M level; involve mandatory attendance on one afternoon per week over the two-semester academic year, a written assignment and the production of a portfolio with evidence of teaching development. Underpinning every component of the course was the principle of 'reflective practice' and the need to interrelate theoretical and practical perspectives on teaching. The early part of the course included 'survival' skills (eg, opening a lecture presentation, using an overhead projector) but progressed quickly as participants became more confident to consider assessment, course design, equal opportunities issues or the application of information technology and multi-media.

Extensive use was made from the start of video-recorded presentations made by the participants to each other in small groups, commendation balancing constructive criticism, and individual staff confidence increased markedly. Evaluations highlighted the value of the mutual peer support network, particularly as this course was often the only occasion where they could meet colleagues in a similar position across other faculties of the university. Comparing experiences also quickly revealed varying practice in schools' staff induction and mentoring programmes and raised expectations among new staff. Participants welcomed, if sometimes apprehensively, the opportunity for class observations both by tutors, subject mentors and peers and they were encouraged to visit experienced colleagues' classes. One new lecturer, for example, who lost his temper in class with a student, was grateful to talk through the experience with his tutor and reflect on alternative strategies for handling difficult situations; in another, the need to improve OHP slides or respond to poor student punctuality were useful issues for discussion. Central to the process was the desire to enhance the students' learning experience.

Another helpful feature of the PGCHE course was the opportunity to develop teaching and learning materials such as study guides or hypercourseware. These materials could then be submitted as part of the participant's written assignment, together with reflections on the development and evaluation process. Student evaluations were also included in the lecturer's portfolio with a view to encouraging developmental rather than judgemental participation and feedback, thereby involving the students more as 'learning partners' (Hibberd, 1993, p.390); it also helped staff and students distinguish between 'good' teaching and merely 'popular' teaching. Just as the PGCHE course facilitated team-teaching, participant interaction and active learning, so this could provide an effective role-model for new lecturers in developing their own good practice. The clarification of learning outcomes for the course offered a useful framework for assessment, again an important example for lecturers to follow in planning their own courses.

Few would object in principle to the need for professional training for academic teachers. Yet the implications of releasing all such new lecturers for at least three hours per week were considerable. On the other hand, newly appointed staff were very appreciative of the opportunity to share their experiences with each other on a weekly basis, to test out their teaching skills, to reflect on their practice and to explore higher level issues in teaching and learning. More than half chose to continue into the second year of the PGCHE programme with one taught unit and a dissertation, despite the pressures of increased course responsibilities. South Bank University allows the weekly PGCHE seminars to be designated part of lecturers' teaching hours during their first academic year and the course encourages them to take back what they have learnt not just into their own classrooms but, perhaps even more importantly, to share with other academic colleagues in their schools and faculties. The opportunity to disseminate and discuss good practice across the university is thereby enhanced.

School staff development

Such opportunities, however, can only be seized if the schools themselves are receptive to new ideas and have structures in place to facilitate such developments. School staff development policies have tended to be preoccupied with the financial implications of sabbatical leave or conference attendance. In 1992, the staff development and appraisal scheme was introduced for all academics across the university, which allowed them the opportunity to discuss their own professional needs and development in research, teaching and administration with a senior colleague on a regular basis. This process provided a valuable channel of communication between staff and encouraged academics to review their own contribution to the quality of university teaching. Each school has identified a senior member of staff to take responsibility for following up the staff development needs both of individuals and the organization.

Colleagues are encouraged to explore innovative approaches to teaching and learning. Mentors assisting new colleagues in their induction to the university come together to discuss the potential of such a role for improving the quality of the new staff's experience of a lively academic community. Increasingly, heads of school/ school senior managers are recognizing the importance of team building, perhaps through whole-school seminars or residentials, so that all staff can be involved in quality enhancement. As Roger Ellis suggests,

> One vital lesson we can learn from quality in industry and health care is that assurance requires a commitment to quality throughout the organisation and works best where all play their part. (1993b, p.17)

Developments in technology

The Teaching and Learning Technology Programme (TLTP), initiated by HEFCE in 1992, aims to make 'teaching and learning more productive and efficient by harnessing modern technology' and to help higher education institutions 'promote and maintain the quality of their provision'. Technology-based approaches can complement more traditional university teaching, create greater flexibility and variety in course programmes and enrich the students' learning experience. As sophisticated computer hardware reduces in both size and cost, software packages or courseware developed by programmes like TLTP, in which South Bank is involved, become more accessible to students and teachers. At the same time, tempting though it may be to leave such initiatives to individual enthusiasts, it is important that all staff are encouraged to undertake computer-based training and given confidence to see the application of technology to enhance the quality of their teaching and administration. This calls for a commitment to staff training such as that recognized by South Bank University's IT training centre which, since it opened in May 1993, has been much appreciated by staff of varying IT capabilities, support and academic, undergoing training from word-processing through to the use of multi-media.

The increasing use of technology by academics has improved the quality of teaching materials (even the simple legibility of overheads); the easier availability and interactive capability of a wide range of resources has provided students with greater opportunities for flexible study and independent learning. The facilities for staff training in technology have made a marked difference to quality.

Student learning

In the desire to support academics in improving the quality of their teaching, it is important not to lose sight of the student learning process: too often teachers focus entirely on their teaching content and method, failing to assess whether the students have learnt what they intended. The expansion in higher education over recent years has also meant a wider range of learning capability in the student intake. In response to these issues, South Bank has enhanced its central support for learning by developing hypercourseware and resource-based learning packages, by establishing a centre for academic learning resources in the newly built library, by promoting a major initiative for supporting dyslexic students and by raising staff awareness of students' general learning needs. Alongside these university-wide developments, individual subject areas have produced additional support materials for students, such as a series of workbooks on mathematics for engineers or an introductory study skills unit for social scientists as part of their BA course. All such initiatives demonstrate to students that South Bank University is committed to encouraging quality in both the teaching and learning process.

Conclusion

Total quality management has been around for many years in industry and opinion is divided on its appropriateness for higher education. The PCFC report on *Teaching Quality* (Warnock, 1990) suggested that 'total quality' corresponds to

the 'ethos' of an institution within which all the staff and the students share the goals of the institution. Yet it is essential to remember that the concepts of industry are no more than metaphors, when applied to higher education, though they may be extremely illuminating. (para 5.8)

What is effective is an institution which takes responsibility for quality on itself by internal self-evaluation. Alongside universities' policies on teaching and learning, curriculum organization and delivery, professional development of staff and student evaluations, an ethos needs to be developed in which the university constantly reflects on the way it operates and the value it places on the quality of its teaching.

Teaching and learning take place in a complex environment where institutional and course procedures overlap and staff and students interact. It is at this interface that quality issues need to be addressed and evaluated. The institutional commitment to quality at South Bank University is evident both through the TQ initiative and its support for academic teaching and learning. Quality is about being accountable to customers, be they students or those outside in the community, through course evaluations, student opinion-surveys or degree results: the university is currently drawing up its own South Bank Charter to clarify the rights and obligations of students.

The emphasis should be on enhancing expertise and empowerment rather than on external mechanisms for control. The inner motivation of academics, their professional commitment to their students, their intellectual love of learning, their respect for peer recognition, in the end are more powerful than any external assessments or mechanistic performance indicators in creating an ethos of total quality in higher education. TQM is after all a commitment, not to instant perfection but to continuous improvement, less about the quantity of statistics than about the quality of relationships; for universities are not ultimately about products but about the development of human beings.

TQM in the classroom

Interestingly, there are accounts of individual teachers in higher education using the strategies of total quality management (or total quality improvement) to help them address the needs of students in just one subject (Hansen, 1993; Hau, 1992). Hau, teaching statistics in a programme which emphasized quality improvement strategies, sought to give his students experience of how they work by forming a quality team of six students who helped him identify potential problem areas for other students, who surveyed the rest of the class to establish priority areas for change, and who monitored improvements after he acted on the information. The process was documented and passed on to a team in the next semester so improvements could be continual. One comment we might make was that although the improvements requested by students might have been important to them, they were primarily informed by the students' apparently teacher-centred notions of learning and did not press the teacher to move toward the conditions we specify as necessary for high quality learning.

Hansen's use of TQI in instruction started with an attempt to define the proficiencies he wished his students to demonstrate on completing study of his subject. He asked employers what they wanted graduates to be able to do and he asked graduates what they valued. The proficiencies (consistent with the characteristics of high quality learning) he defined were:

- gaining access to existing knowledge
- displaying command of existing knowledge
- displaying the ability to draw out knowledge
- utilizing it to explore issues
- creating new knowledge.

In one semester he became particularly concerned with addressing the fifth proficiency, so he formed research teams to investigate questions to which there were no ready-made answers. One of the teams monitored the subject itself and the success of the teaching strategies, in particular the team projects and how they were managed. The focus on the 'customer' typical of TQI is apparent in defining the proficiencies; participation is satisfied through the students' involvement in teams, including the monitoring team; and continuous improvement is achieved as the teacher acts on the information obtained one semester to improve the experience for both current and future students.

Doubts about TQM

So far we have concentrated on the positive in this review of the potential of action research and/or TQM as strategies – in our view strategies which share many similarities – which might enable universities gradually to reshape themselves into learning organizations in which all categories of staff work to achieve institutional goals and, in particular, the goal of fostering high quality student learning. We have already noted that the dramatic change Argyris and Schön try to promote does not happen rapidly, nor would a group of action research projects coalesce quickly to create a new culture within a university. Are there any published accounts of failed projects which may help us plan for success?

Miller and Cangemi (1993) describe how United States industry has struggled to implement TQM, employee and customer dissatisfaction, and continuing costly levels of error. First of all, for success of a full-scale programme there must be a massive change in the climate of most organizations. Everyone must accept responsibility for quality, but on the other side of the coin, everyone must be involved in making decisions about changes to processes and empowered to implement them. It is very difficult for managers brought up in a different tradition of management to relinquish control to workers, to cease allocating blame when something goes wrong and instead praise when the error is corrected, and to stop buck-passing and accept responsibility themselves. Communications between all levels of the organization must be free, open and honest, and that is a goal very difficult to achieve in the individualistic, incentive-driven workforce to which we are accustomed.

Second, the programme cannot be entrusted to a few; it must be instituted and supported constantly by everyone, especially those at the top of the organization. Without that commitment, programmes just peter out instead of creating a whole new way of operating within the organization, a habit of quality.

Third, the organization needs to be able to demonstrate that the quality programme is having an effect, that there is measurable improvement. The other side of this coin is the urge to create a bureaucracy to monitor the quality programme which may divert energy from quality improvement to bean-counting – a danger higher education institutions are well aware of as they are required to provide more and more data to governments which frequently either misinterpret or ignore it.

Watkins (1993) surveys various views of TQM from the perspective of higher education. He notes the widely held view that it is potentially a very congenial and appropriate way of working toward the goals of higher education, but he also cites the work of others who have found it to be oppressive rather than empowering for workers. The argument is that

> ...while TQM does encourage the decentralisation of responsibilities which were traditionally held centrally, this does not necessarily lead to greater autonomy. Rather the result is that employees are asked to perform an increasing number of tasks which are, in turn, closely monitored and strictly controlled. The characteristic of TQM regimes is the extension of management control with work intensified through heightened surveillance, accountability, peer pressure and waste elimination. (p.13)

Thus, while we can see many attractions in the principles of TQM in trying to bring about some changes in our own institutions, we would prefer to start with facilitation of action research projects. It seems to us that learning how to engage in the cycle of planning, acting, observing and reflecting in a systematic and thoughtful way would be an excellent way to begin to understand how TQM *should* work. In the final chapter of *Action Research in Higher Education: Examples and reflections*, Zuber-Skerritt (1992b) engages in a personal reflection on her own facilitation of action research to improve practice in higher education. Making explicit the parallel between staff learning in such a project and the best practice in promoting student learning, she concludes:

> My reflections on this case lead me to the conclusion that my role as an educational adviser in higher education is not so much to provide information, advice and the results of evaluation and research to teaching staff who would then apply this knowledge to their practice, but to help them to create this knowledge themselves through experience, self-reflection and critical debate with others. Similarly, the role of teaching staff is not so much to provide students with the answers of their research in a particular field, but with questions which give them the opportunity to discover the answers themselves through problem-solving and discussion with their fellow students and staff. (p.107)

Conclusion

One appealing aspect of the ambitious attempts to introduce TQM throughout a university, as has been done at South Bank (Chadwick in this chapter; Geddes, 1993a), Wolverhampton (Doherty, 1993), Miami-Dade Community College (Badley, 1992) and Oregon State University (Coate, 1993), is the explicit recognition that every single section of the university contributes to the quality of teaching and learning which takes place in that institution. The notion of a quality chain (Geddes, 1993a) in which there are internal customers of services of different divisions of the institution as well as external customers is extremely attractive to those of us who emphasize the community of quality. Another is the inclusion of participants in the system from outside the institution in the TQM processes. For too long attention has been directed solely on the role of the teacher in promoting high quality learning and, particularly in the old universities where course design has not been so rigorously monitored as in the former polytechnics and colleges of advanced education, for too long the classroom performance aspect of teaching has received undue prominence.

What is required is a 'community of quality'. If the so-called quality debate is to move past hollow public rhetoric, we believe it is essential to readjust our image of universities and recognize them as complex organizations within a very complex system. The traditional image of academics who occasionally teach classes surrounded by support staff who deal with the mundane matters of enrolment and record-keeping has never been valid, but the 'them and us' culture on most campuses has and will continue to limit the ability of the institutions to meet the multiplicity of challenges being thrown at them. In addition, there has been some truth in the description of academic departments as fiefdoms at war with each other in the battle for scarce resources. In the most instrumental terms, the very survival of the institutions, not to mention their ability to offer high quality learning experiences, may very well be dependent on their ability to mobilize their considerable internal resources and to engage in productive collaboration with external stakeholders to work for the benefit of the whole system.

Middlehurst (1992, pp.34–5) outlines some of the connotations of taking quality as an organizing principle for an institution:

> Firstly, ... quality should become the fundamental concept around which institutional activity is focused and measured and the means by which institutional (and individual) priorities are established. ... Secondly, ...'quality' can serve to bring together all parts and operations of the institution into an organic whole, establishing co-operation between elements in order to achieve the central focus on quality. Thirdly, the idea of an organising principle implies the provision of an orderly structure, a framework which relates elements to each other and establishes a working order for the achievement of quality.

She notes that private sector total quality management programmes are built around these implications of taking quality as an organizing principle, but that they also 'resonate with higher education traditions of collegiality or professionalism'. At the conclusion of her paper, she also explicitly draws the parallel between the basic requirements of programmes for quality enhancement and the requirements of learning programmes – 'clarity of purpose, feedback on performance and constant effort to develop and improve'. Again there is a parallel between the needs of the learners and the requirements of quality enhancement: after all, to improve continuously one must be learning continuously.

Chapter 8

Judging Quality Outcomes

We hope that defining one overarching purpose of all higher education will unite stakeholders in some sense of common purpose. We hope that stakeholders can agree at least with the thrust of our characterization of high quality learning and to work, as a community of quality, toward the conditions in which high quality learning is likely to occur.

We have proposed a strategy and some specific tactics via case studies, for working toward achievement of the vision. The strategy is congruent with our understanding of the optimal conditions for individual and organizational learning which we believe will be necessary throughout the community. In passing, we have pointed out some attempts to assure quality which we believe could be counter-productive. Now we must address the serious question of accountability. We accept that the universities must be accountable to the other stakeholders, but we will assert again that accountability is mutual.

It seems to us that to begin we should, once again, step back from the arguments over details – performance indicators and audit units and so on – and try for a moment to get a grip on the main issue. If our goal is to foster higher order intellectual capabilities, how can we know we have achieved the goal? Is it possible to specify and assess these capabilities in such a way that both intramural and extramural stakeholders have some evidence that high quality learning is taking place? We believe it is.

The first step toward accountability: processes

Programmes of study are organized in many different ways. The majority use subjects as building blocks of programmes but there are increasing numbers of programmes offered in modules. Nevertheless, there is some sort of unit and someone responsible for it (subject convenor, programme team). One simple way of beginning a programme of quality assurance is to ask those responsible for the basic units which characteristics of high quality learning they are trying to foster, how they do it, and how they know the students can do what is necessary. The subject convenor of Building Economics I might answer that she is concerned about students' ability to use the library resources effectively (part of being able to discover knowledge for oneself), so together with the reader services librarian she offers students instruction in research skills, specifically the use of various abstracting services and bibliographies relevant to the discipline of economics. Because she knows that skills are best learned when they are being applied, this instruction is part of the process of guiding students through the writing of their first essay in the subject, so she is also addressing 'being able to communicate knowledge'. Because she is also aware of the threat to high quality learning posed by anxiety and that first-year students writing their first essay in an unfamiliar subject may be unready both cognitively and emotionally for the task, she uses workshop techniques to help students discover what they already know which is relevant to the topic (also creating conditions for relating previous knowledge to new and being active); workshops also give students an opportunity to talk through ideas with each other and share the results of their reading, and she makes sure that they have feedback on a draft (at least from classmates if she cannot provide it) before the essay is finally assessed. In an effort to reduce anxiety about the assessment, she allows students whose first submission does not meet her clearly articulated criteria – which in this case emphasize demonstrating that they were able to discover a wide range of material on the topic and present it in a clear and logical order – to resubmit their essays. (A personal comment: this description is based on the practice of teachers whose work we know well.)

This first step, asking which characteristics of high quality learning the teacher is emphasizing and how she is establishing the conditions under which it is likely to occur, is taken within departments. The next step is to ask those responsible for programmes of study – degree courses or any other sequence or collection of units – whether the programme consciously addresses all characteristics and what it does to ensure that the necessary conditions exist. We would expect faculties (or schools or departments) to respond to these questions within the institution, but we would expect their responses to be in the public domain, available to any stakeholder who wanted detail as, in fact, should be subject teachers' reports.

Institutions also should address these questions, by ensuring that they are asked in detail at subject level at the time of approval of new programmes or modification of existing programmes and at the time of evaluation of programmes. Every programme should be evaluated regularly and in line with best practice in evaluation. (Specific recommendations for programme evaluation are available in many published resources. See, for instance, O'Neil and Pennington, 1992; Ramsden and Dodds, 1989; Roe and McDonald, 1983; Roe et al., 1986.) Institutions should also be able to report what is done at institutional level to ensure that the necessary conditions for high quality learning are provided. At this level resources and services will figure prominently in the account, as will staff development opportunities and the results of review cycles.

These suggestions are not different from common practice in most institutions of higher education except for our emphasis on the characteristics and conditions as a way of focusing attention on what (we believe) really matters. Reviewing recommendations from various stakeholders about accountability or improving higher education reveals a lot of trees but no sense of the forest. Stepping back to rediscover the forest would allow the whole system, first, to simplify the processes and, second, to make them more effective. Asking the wrong questions in the wrong way in the name of accountability is likely to impede rather than improve high quality learning. For instance, think again of the cases Gibbs (1992b) cites in which students reject the innovations designed to encourage high quality learning in favour of the easy-way-out, teacher-centred methods with which they are familiar.

Remembering Barnett's (1992a, Chapter 2) point that the aims of higher education are achieved by the students, not by the teachers or the administrators, we must admit that none of the suggestions above guarantees the desired outcome of high quality learning, nor do they make it possible to report to stakeholders that it is being achieved. So far all that can be reported is that the institution is addressing specifically the characteristics and creating the necessary conditions. This should make the desired outcomes more likely but there is no guarantee since the learning remains in the students' hands.

One way out of the quandary is to quit here and agree to judge the quality of the processes but not the outcome. That is too easy and too much of a total abdication of responsibility for everyone, including the students. They are part of the community of quality and they, too, are accountable.

The second step toward accountability: outcomes

The one certain way of discovering whether students are achieving high quality learning is through assessment (if it actually assesses the achievement of high quality learning objectives). Once again the level of the teaching unit is the key. (Note: we still believe the whole community of quality shares responsibility, but teachers are in the front line.) If assessment tasks require students to do things which demonstrate that they are capable of the type of learning that we have characterized as high quality and if they succeed in those tasks, we have evidence of high quality learning.

There is another side to the assessment coin. Student learning research has repeatedly demonstrated the impact of assessment on students' approaches to learning (see Biggs, 1989; Gibbs, 1992a, 1992b; Ramsden, 1988). Ask them to understand the physics and chemistry of muscle contraction, but test them on the names of the muscles, and they will 'learn' the names but not be able to explain how contraction happens. Ask students to understand narrative perspective in the novel but test them on the author's background and they will know a lot about the author and little about narrative perspective.

A mini case study on assessment – anonymous

A story to illustrate how easy it is for things to go wrong when it comes to assessment: a lecturer in a behavioural sciences subject (second year of a three-year Bachelors degree programme) wanted his students to learn the rudiments of the research process. He set them the task of identifying a question they wished to research (something in the area of the subject's content, of course), reviewing the literature, designing a project, conducting it and reporting on it. This was the only assessable work for the half-year subject. Class meetings were designed to support the students through the process, teaching them how to do each step. So far he is creating many of the conditions for encouraging high quality learning: letting the students choose work which matters to them so it will build on their experience, be seen as relevant, etc; high level of activity as they learn both content and skills; interaction with others; and support for the process.

One student made a slow start to her project, failed the review of the literature stage, passed the project design stage but without distinction and then got deeply involved in what she was doing. She executed a very challenging project, became very excited about what she learned and was even being encouraged by another member of staff to think about combining her work with some of the staff member's for a joint publication. At the stage where she had to write the final report which was supposed to be weighted very heavily in determining a final grade in the subject, she learned from a third-year student that the lecturer had a policy of not awarding a grade higher than a pass to anyone who failed any element of the assessment in the subject. She did minimal work on the final report and got the passing grade but not the high grade she could have got for the work if the policy had been different. She put extra time into memorizing a set of formulae in preparation for an examination in a subject which bored her, achieved a very high grade on the exam and in the subject, and promptly forgot all the formulae.

The lecturer's espoused theory was that students should learn by doing, which he said meant learning from their mistakes, but his assessment policy said that mistakes are punished. He explained his policy as necessary to force students to take the process seriously, but he never even knew what he had sacrificed. The student never completed the learning from her project work and did not achieve the final insight into results that comes from the hard work of putting all the pieces together. What is probably worse, she learned that if you do not toe the line, if you do make mistakes, no amount of excellent work compensates (see Dunlap, 1990, for an excellent account of the results of students' receiving many messages like this – unwillingness to take intellectual risks, be creative, seek alternative explanations, etc). She also learned that surface learning is rewarded.

There is a postscript to this story as well. Another student who achieved a high grade for the project report was very disappointed to receive only a pass for the subject. When she inquired, she was shown how the grades were 'added up' and that her early work 'brought down' her average. Angry and upset, she recognized that she was being punished for learning from her mistakes, but she did not point out this inconsistency to the teacher, nor would she seek advice or mediation from anyone else in the department. She was afraid that the teacher would 'make her life miserable' in the second half of the year when she would be enrolled in another subject he taught. Had he been involved in a collaborative process with participants, such as action research or TQI in the classroom, the teacher might have learned something from his own mistake. It might have been prevented in the first place if he had consulted with students to develop an assessment policy.

Not only does good assessment practice *demonstrate* high quality learning but also good assessment practice is likely to *encourage* high quality learning. However, here is another point of shared responsibility for quality; teachers are reporting that with larger classes and fewer teachers, methods of assessment are moving back towards those which do not encourage high quality learning. While some strategies for doing more with less may be suggested (see Andresen *et al.*, 1992), there is a point at which the overload cannot be reconciled with good practice. The funding of higher education is not the responsibility of the institutions; for this, government must be held accountable.

An outcomes-centred project

Interestingly, a project focusing on learning outcomes, but working from a different perspective, also found assessment to take on a much more important role than participants expected at the beginning of the project. The Unit for the Development of Continuing Adult Education (UDACE) (now part of the Further Education Unit) asked academics in five subject areas 'to define the outcomes of existing degree programmes and examine approaches to assessing and accrediting those outcomes' (Otter, 1992, p.iii). Although the subject area teams were given various materials to assist their work, they were not given a single model of how to go about their task. One of the objectives of the project was to test and refine a collaborative model for the development of learning outcome statements, an objective which was achieved though each team worked differently.

As the teams worked, they approached describing learning outcomes for degree courses from four different perspectives:

Objectives	the stated intentions of the course
Subject knowledge	the knowledge content commonly identified in syllabuses or course documentation
Discipline	the notion of a discipline as a culture and value system to which the graduate is admitted
Competence	what a graduate can do as a result of the degree programme, including the narrower notion of occupational competence. (p.15)

If one reconsiders the characteristics of high quality learning (see Chapter 4), implicit in each statement is a broad competence. While we suggest that focusing on that description of the characteristics of high quality learning may help gain some perspective on making judgements of quality in higher education, that approach would not be sufficient for the purposes of developing courses or evaluating them in regular cycles of programme review. For those purposes, one must be a great deal more specific, detailing subject content which must be mastered, the concepts and methodologies that inform the discipline, specific competences and personal values expected of a graduate of such a course, and so on. Among other things, the UDACE project has demonstrated that:

- it is possible to describe the outcomes of higher education more explicitly, although they cannot be expressed in simple 'can do' statements, and in a complex and changing environment, such definitions will never be complete or fixed;
- descriptions of learning outcomes in higher education cannot be expressed as a single set of 'national standards' of the kind developed for National Vocational Qualifications, since higher education exists to meet the needs of a variety of client groups and a range of social, economic, scientific and actual needs, and properly embodies a range of different cultures and value systems;
- it is necessary to develop processes within each institution to link outcome definitions with quality assurance, since the authority to define the purposes of degree programmes rests with the chartered institution, rather than with any national agency. (p.79)

Chapter 8 of Otter's report offers 'A Model for Quality' (see Figure 8.1) which can be seen as a particular instance of the general strategy for improving quality which we have linked to action research leading to both individual and organizational learning.

In the first stage academic staff go through the very difficult process of describing the outcomes of a degree course. It is an 'iterative and collaborative process which seeks to make more explicit the many implicit

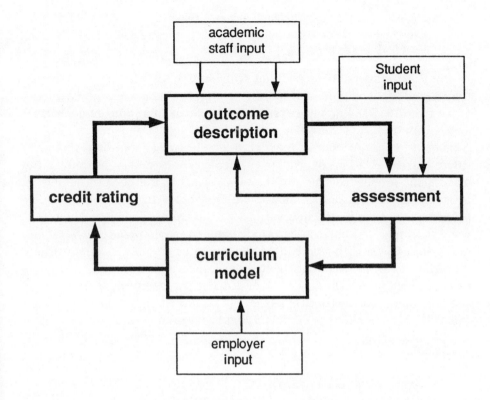

Figure 8.1 *A model for quality (Otter, 1992)*

outcomes expected of a graduate of a given programme' (p.93). In the second stage staff work out how those outcomes will be assessed; they seek student input at this stage. The result of linking outcomes and assessment was more than simply being able to demonstrate that outcomes would be achieved. The discussions among staff and students led to clarification of the outcomes themselves and redrafting; students developed much better understanding of expected outcomes; and staff had to examine the validity of assessment methods they had previously taken for granted. The key conclusions of the project relating to assessment were:

- the definition of outcomes should not be separated from an investigation of assessment since outcome definitions which are not assessable are not of any practical value;
- an outcome led approach requires staff to develop and use methods of assessment which measure achievements directly, but current assessment practice tends to neglect these questions of validity in favour of reliability, and many academic staff lack experience of appropriate approaches to assessment;

- students can play a particularly valuable role in the development of approaches to assessment, and this dialogue can itself help to increase their motivation and advisement. (pp.79–80)

In the third stage staff, consulting with employers, shape 'a potentially fragmented list of outcomes, of varying sizes and kinds, into a coherent model of the award' (p.94). Employers proved helpful in defining core outcomes and appropriate balances between subject knowledge, discipline values and competences but, of course, they were also learning – not only about the values and expectations of academics but also about student learning as the discussions proceeded. The fourth stage relates to the need to be able to accumulate and transfer credit for different types of learning into other programmes of study and into various vocational qualification schemes. It was not always possible to assign credit value to groups of outcomes, though the attempt to clarify how credit could be granted resulted in more learning for academic staff who had been little concerned with such issues as recognition of prior experience and alternative paths to degrees.

This project provides both considerable insight into how higher education can meet demands for accountability and an example of a process which results in learning about high quality learning by various stakeholders. In Otter's words:

the principal benefit in an outcomes led approach lies, therefore, in providing a focus for staff, students and employers to examine more clearly what they are seeking to achieve, and in enabling them to contribute actively to the development of a common understanding of the nature and purposes of higher education and of specific programmes and awards. (p.79)

CASE STUDY

An Outcomes Approach to a Degree Programme

Mike O'Neil and Ken Onion, Nottingham Trent University

In 1992–3 the faculty of education at Nottingham Trent University created a new degree course based upon an outcomes approach. The document which was prepared by the planning team to secure course approval was long and complex and extensive use is made of extracts from the validated documents to give the most direct insight into some of the major issues confronted by the planning group and into the ways in which they attempted to deal with them to the satisfaction of a validating panel which consisted of internal and external academics, employers and managers. The course has yet to take its first students so the evaluation of this 'outcomes approach' to learning practice and skill development is some way in the future.

The initiative for a new BA course arose from the interests and expertise of a group of staff in the faculty of education. The group shared the view of employing organizations and government that underpinning many professional and occupational activities is a central core of 'competences'. The decision to plan a whole degree programme based on an outcomes model was reached early in the planning process. The group paid particular attention to the work of Otter (1992) and Biggs and Collis (1982) because these analyses drew the same general conclusion of those expressed by the planning group: that it was important to engage with the 'observable' domain of what students actually do. This simplifies the process of assessment and enables a student's achievements to be communicated in clear terms to prospective employers. Otter's work in particular – and her presence in the same university – enabled the team to benefit from her enquiries and to catch her energy and enthusiasm for an outcomes model.

It was far less easy to conceptualize outcome in specific terms. While the team were convinced that a range of competences could be identified, promoted and assessed, the term 'competence' had connotations which the team wished to avoid. In addition, the team were also convinced that a 'content-light' curriculum is neither interesting nor should it be part of the mission of the university: a university is a community of scholars who have a commitment to the generation and dissemination of knowledge. Further, competences or skills are always anchored in a context of meaning. Accordingly, after a great deal of discussion about alternative conceptualizations, the group decided to formulate two sorts of outcomes: general outcomes and knowledge outcomes. The details of and reasons for making this distinction are outlined later in the case study.

Another early, strategic decision was to keep the number of outcomes to a manageable level. To this end, the team articulated five general outcomes (see below) which would penetrate all course clusters and all course modules. (Note: 'clusters' are optional routes through the degree.) Rules about 'progression' in the outcomes were also devised early on in the curriculum planning cycle (briefly set out below, following the description of each outcome).

All of the group who planned this degree were closely involved with the Enterprise in Higher Education (EHE) Initiative (see Macnair, 1990; Wright, 1992) and had considerable experience in educational development. Consequently, they were keen to try to bridge the apparent gap between a vocationally relevant degree and one maintaining a more traditional academic orientation. As it turned out, these philosophies were not mutually antagonistic: the link between them centred on the interconnectedness of the ideas and practice associated with a 'deep' approach to learning (see Chapters 4 and 5) *and* the skill requirements of the workplace, which has been well argued by Stephenson and Weil (1992) on behalf of the RSA's 'Higher Education for Capability Campaign'.

The rest of this account is intended to provide a brief overview of the notion of outcomes, as the team operationalized it, and to explain some of the associated language and ideas which are used in the degree document.

A degree course which is based on outcomes is attractive for many reasons. Such a model:

- enables the graduate and the employer to know what the student has actually accomplished in specific and mutually intelligible terms;
- enables closer integration of the course and previous work experience;
- shifts the focus of course delivery away from classroom learning to tasks at hand. This immediately provides a rationale in which the attainment of outcomes can be achieved in a variety of ways and settings;
- concentrates the minds of design teams to think carefully about what exactly it is their modules intend to achieve;
- requires very close attention to the structure and mechanism of assessment. It also means that those who write modules have to be clear about how their assessment contributes to the students' overall programme.

Just before the degree document was finalized the university produced for all staff a document *Describing Learning Outcomes* (DLO) which provided a clear outline of the concept of outcome and some of its intellectual and practical implications. The concept is not new. The planning group had been impressed particularly by the work at Alverno State College in the United States which has, since the early 1970s, organized its entire undergraduate provision on an outcomes model.

'Learning outcomes are descriptions of what a student must know and be able to do in order to satisfy the requirements of a module and to gain credits' (DLO). The university paper describes three kinds of outcome:

- knowledge outcomes, which 'describe how students will be able to demonstrate the knowledge they have gained';
- skills and personal competences which 'can be personal, intellectual and social';
- personal competences which are 'concerned with attitudes, beliefs and dispositions'.

The design team were uneasy about how far it is possible to distinguish knowledge outcomes from general outcomes in a satisfactory way. For instance, a *communication* is not satisfactory if the information which is relayed is ill-informed or betrays serious weaknesses of understanding. Nevertheless, the distinction between knowledge outcomes and general outcomes has considerable pragmatic value. The degree's knowledge outcomes consist of a range of accomplishments of a kind familiar to most academics and which form the basis of most assessments on degree courses. Increasingly, students who come to the university from school or college will be familiar with both sorts of outcomes. The group were happy to use the distinction because they believe that its intelligibility is of great value at this stage in the development of higher education and one of the central tasks of the members of the team responsible for this degree will be to contribute their own experiences, ideas and research to the wider debate about the conceptual and practical relationships between these two kinds of outcomes.

Outcomes defined for the BA in human and education studies

General outcomes

Five were ultimately selected. They are:

communication
problem solving
interpersonal relationships
planning and strategic thinking
visioning/evaluating/critiquing.

The team were aware that to have more than six or seven general outcomes leads to excessive complexity in the course design. Whenever possible they opted for simplicity when planning the course. The outcomes were subjected to a conceptual analysis. Below is a brief sketch of how each of these outcomes is seen by the course team. The degree planning group believe that the general outcomes will actively foster in students lively, practical competences in the following areas.

Communication   This refers to speaking clearly, precisely and confidently; being sensitive to, and being able to use, different modes of communication according to the needs of the audience; being able to interpret the significance of communications from other people.

Progression within this outcome is defined in terms of the development of competence in different forms of communication including oral, written and graphical, as well as the delivery of more complex content; the application of the different forms of communication skills to a widening range of audiences, from small informal groups to larger groups of individuals; and the development of fluency and sophistication in communicating.

Problem solving   This entails skills in being able to appraise and analyse situations; being able to employ critical skills in order to generate problem-solving strategies; being able to draw upon and justify appropriate human and material resources; being able to accept responsibility for decisions made.

Progression within this outcome can be defined as competence in dealing with problems of increasing size, in terms of the number of variables involved in the problem, and of increasing complexity of context, which could range from a relatively clear, simple situation to one which is ambiguous and more complex.

It is recognized that students will require the opportunity for development of a wide range of skills which are necessary components for competence within this area, for example:

- data gathering techniques;
- strategies for the interpretation of data;
- the ability to apply data to specific contexts and to articulate solutions.

Development is also seen to involve, *inter alia,* being able to articulate the elements of the problem, to define problems using a theoretical framework and an ability to articulate the processes of problem solution adopted, towards the inclusion of others within that framework, and evaluating the relative effectiveness of different problem-solving approaches.

Interpersonal relationships   This involves competence in being able to recognize one's strengths and weaknesses and those of others; being able to act as a catalyst, coordinator, facilitator, evaluator, monitor, while working in groups; being able to defuse conflict constructively; being able to assume responsibility for working with and through other people. Cooperation rather than conflict contributes significantly to morale and productivity in all organizations that graduates are likely to work in.

Progression within this area is seen to involve the development of the ability to identify one's own behaviour when interacting in small groups. Development would also involve the ability to operate effectively in groups of different sizes and types within a variety of contexts, and the ability to fulfil a variety of roles within groups involving the application of leadership and management skills.

Planning and strategic thinking   This describes competence in being able to set and achieve meaningful goals in both personal and professional settings; being able to envisage situations and to develop contingency plans; being able to frame priorities and to coordinate and schedule accordingly; being able to reflect upon the predicted and actual outcomes of an action plan.

Progression within this area is seen to involve dealing with one's own planning, implementation and evaluation of actions, and the inclusion of others within that planning process. Development will involve fulfilling increasingly complex roles in differing sizes and types of group setting, dealing with more complex situations, involving the need to deal with a longer time scale and with conflict and ambiguity, the recognition and positive response to change in self.

Visioning/evaluating/critiquing   The design group could find no single English word which encapsulates what they mean. The clumsy, ugly phrase they were left with refers to a set of competences dealing with how people are able to move their thoughts, plans and actions from the present to the future. It entails evaluating past actions with a view to incorporating lessons learned into future action plans; showing positive responses to change and responding appropriately to appraisals provided by other people; taking risks, persevering in the face of obstacles and being prepared to learn from mistakes and successes; developing a vision of the future and being able to communicate this in ways which enable others to share it.

Progression within this area would involve the development of the ability to adopt an analytical and reflective approach to the evaluation of one's own and others' actions, incorporating increasingly complex concepts and theories within the analysis and involving the recognition and criticism of paradigms; and to consider creative solutions to both new and old dilemmas.

Assessment of learning outcomes: two examples

The course team determined that the assessment of learning through a 'competences' approach was a major challenge and were concerned to avoid assessing outcomes in a similar manner to the way in which occupational competences are assessed in the UK through NVQs; that is, on a 'Yes/No' or 'can do' basis.

All courses either explicitly or implicitly assess objectives, that is the knowledge, skills and attitudes of their students. For example the marking of essays often refers to such features as the structure, the clarity of writing, extent of analysis and the use of the literature. All of those can and should be expressed as objectives or outcomes, for outcomes have essentially a similar meaning as objectives. In this course the intention is to very explicitly assess outcomes and indeed to make a feature of it. In doing so the stance is not atypical but rather a question of emphasis.

The kinds of general outcomes to be assessed were therefore embedded in the knowledge outcomes associated with each module. As an illustration of this principle, the assessment of two modules is given here: assessment of a social and personal issues module (P110) and assessment of a technology and environmental issues module (T230). (NB: the general outcome component is in *italic*; the knowledge outcome component is in normal font.)

Learning outcomes of 'Personality and learning' module P110

At the end of this module the student will be able to:

1. *explain* the essential elements of psychometric and humanistic theories of personality and the different approaches to and styles of learning;
2. *appraise and value* the different methods of personality assessment and be able *to recognize* the strengths and weaknesses of these different methods;
3. *recognize the importance of different approaches and roles* in learning, namely: active/passive learning; experiential learning; learning styles and approaches; independent and open learning;
4. *set and achieve meaningful goals and objectives* in relation to a small scale enquiry;
5. *respond to advice and guidance* provided by significant others in the design of an investigation and the preparation of a talk and a report;
6. *speak with confidence to an audience of their peers* about the results of their enquiry;

7. *produce a report of an investigation* into an aspect of how adults differ in personality and in approach to learning, conducted according to a justified ethical position and validated through the use of a triangulation process.

An example of an assessment task Working in small groups, students will be asked to design and conduct a small-scale enquiry into an aspect of how adults differ in personality and in approaches to learning. They will, as a group, present their findings to the class as a whole. In addition, each individual will present an analytic report of their enquiry for self- and tutor assessment.

Learning outcomes of 'Design, technology and innovation' module T230

At the end of this module students will be able to:

1. *speak with confidence and enthusiasm* about design issues and concepts;
2. *use appropriate media to convey information* about innovation and creativity in different cultural and social contexts;
3. *exercise analytical skills to determine the structure* of a design problem;
4. *be creative* and *develop sensitivity to influences of values and beliefs* when evaluating the effectiveness of a product in meeting its declared purpose;
5. *respond positively to change, take risks and learn from the mistakes and successes of self and others* when critically examining the function of a product.

An example of an assessment task Students will be asked to identify, evaluate and re-model an existing technological product designed for a community context, eg, equipment used in an adventure playground, a shopping centre, or a leisure facility; devices or systems for helping the handicapped; communication or transportation systems; security devices or equipment. The evaluation will focus on the product's design function, ergonomics and aesthetics. The model will be supported by evidence of design analysis and justification for the changes proposed.

Final observations

There are dangers in the use of outcomes. The most serious which the group identified are that assessment is reduced to a series of ticks in boxes; that little attention is paid to progression; and that a preoccupation with general outcomes comes to obscure the development of students' achievement of knowledge outcomes.

A further worry experienced by the planning group is that 'outcomes' has sometimes the ring of behaviourist psychology: that to promote outcomes is to dam the imagination and creativity which people possess. This is one of the central and oldest dilemmas in the whole of education. On the one hand, employers, the government and individuals wish children and students to be 'prepared'. As educationists, the group knew from research and from a very wide range of experience that people need the challenge of the unexpected and the stimulation which arises from the imagination being exercised in order to persist in and to benefit from education. On the other hand, most students find it helpful to have targets clearly defined – and to have the rationale which underpins the definition explained and indeed negotiated. The degree proposal therefore strikes a deliberate balance. The outcomes are defined but one of them, 'visioning/evaluating/critiquing', engages explicitly with the unexpected. The course processes are deliberately intended to challenge students and to encourage them to question constantly what they are doing and why. Of course, unexpected things will happen; students will grow in directions that have not been planned for. The team believe that they have sufficient flexibility and imagination to respond positively to such developments, to celebrate them and to learn from them.

In general, progression in learning is seen to entail a shift in outcomes from simple, relatively undifferentiated activities towards those which are more complex and which embrace a larger number of variables.

It is a clear policy to assess general outcomes and knowledge outcomes in each module. As members of a university we have a clear commitment to promoting knowledge. The aims of the course reflect this and the content and arrangement of the modules have been designed to do this.

An embryonic project on assessing outcomes

A team based in the Professional Development Centre of the University of New South Wales (UNSW) has been commissioned by the Committee for the Advancement of University Teaching (CAUT is funded by the Australian Department of Employment, Education and Training) to develop a set of materials to assist academic staff to employ best practice in assessing and examining students. The project is in its very early stages as we complete this book, but of relevance to our discussion is the approach being taken, and since Peggy Nightingale is a member of the team, we are in a position to discuss what she has already learned about attempts to identify goals and aims of higher education.

The team will identify abilities teachers want students to possess at the completion of subjects/modules and courses/programmes. The materials will offer strategies for assessing those abilities, including some alternatives people might not consider such as (perhaps) objective testing of critical thinking. It is intended that each section of the final product will focus on an ability and present a case study of practice in trying to assess that ability, analysis of the case, discussion of alternative assessment techniques and advice about implementation.

That is the current intention, at least. We believe it important to acknowledge that it is not easy to put into words outcomes which are complex and interrelated. We have been arguing for trying to get the discussions of quality back to fundamentals, but we do not want anyone to think that we are not aware of just how hard our approach may be to implement. For instance, the project team at UNSW struggled to choose the word 'ability' rather than 'skill', 'competence', 'capability', etc. just to have a shared vocabulary and understanding among themselves about what it is they are trying to focus on. The team is continuing to struggle to come up with a preliminary list of verbs which express the range of abilities they believe teachers in higher education want and need to assess. The preliminary list will be used to solicit case study examples of assessment practice and to invite teachers to add abilities or suggest better words to name them. As it stands, the preliminary list is:

Knowledge		Professional/technical work-related skills	Higher order
Recognize	– facts	Diagnose	Think critically
Recall	– concepts	Use	Solve problems
Relate (interrelate)	– ideas	Do routine analysis, computation	Communicate effectively
Organize	– terminology	Make	Manage information
Recount (tell someone)	– definitions	Make judgement	Work cooperatively
		Access information	Design – create
		Apply ethical values	Work independently (operate autonomously)
			Evaluate

The assessment project team hopes that eventually through an iterative process and much discussion with teachers in many disciplines they will be able to offer materials centred on abilities which will resonate with the experience of teachers in all disciplines. Perhaps the verbs will give those discipline specialists a starting place for delineating the desired outcomes of their subjects and programmes of study, but each teacher and each programme will have to make specific the outcomes they seek. Simply saying students should recognize facts and recall concepts or communicate effectively will not be enough; the teachers will have to specify which facts and what concepts and what sort of communication to what standard, and so on and on.

Do we need performance indicators?

If quality assurance in higher education were to focus on outcomes and their assessment – on the broad general outcomes implicit in the characteristics of high quality learning for purposes of accountability, and on the detailed statement of outcomes and assessment practices required for programme planning and evaluation – would it be necessary to collect more evidence? For instance, should there be surveys of students at the time of or shortly after graduation? Should there be surveys of employers? There may be public relations reasons for such exercises, but they are unlikely to add much to what is already being learned from the involvement of students and employers in the discussions of outcomes and assessment and from other collaborations on developmental projects within the university. The data collected by such surveys are, of necessity, very non-specific. In addition, such surveys may measure satisfaction but they do not necessarily reveal quality. People may well be satisfied with a very average programme simply because that is all they know. We would argue that if the simple yardstick were applied – 'How does this activity ensure that the conditions for high quality learning are being created?' – the answer would be that it does little or nothing and the resources should be expended in some more constructive way.

However, focusing on assessment of specified outcomes does not reveal why outcomes are not achieved. If there is a high failure rate in a subject, or if the number of first class honours awards is disproportionately low in one degree programme, what is going on? Performance indicators such as distributions of grades, rates of student progress, staff:student ratios, expenditure per student, and so on may raise questions or suggest areas that need investigation; they are necessary for those purposes, but they are not, in themselves, measures of quality. The problem with the attempts to use performance indicators to reward institutions for quality is that a tool is being confused with a result. In addition, some demands for more and more data from the institutions are the result of making the basic mistake of collecting data simply because they are there, not because they will contribute anything significant to what is already known. In this case, too, asking the simple question about how these data make it more likely that the conditions for high quality learning will be satisfied may help reduce wasted time and energy which should be redirected toward action research projects – or TQM projects – aimed at identifying and solving the problems that do impede the achievement of the overarching goal of all higher education and the other goals of each institution.

Chapter 9

Towards a Community of Quality

In looking at quality enhancement across the university system, one recurrent issue is the need for individual and collective action to bring about a 'community of quality', a networked collaborating group of stakeholders dedicated to creating the conditions necessary for high quality learning, enabling students to 'form and substantiate independent thought and action in a coherent and articulate fashion' (Barnett, 1992a, p.58). In this chapter we suggest some initiatives which may encourage this collective action. These suggestions are tentative in the sense that they require translating to suit the contexts within which they may be employed: the different histories, goals and priorities of individuals, institutions and communities must be taken into account.

Because we believe that the higher education system, including all stakeholders (students, all staff, employers, professional bodies, governments, at a minimum), must be dedicated to a conception of quality which is primarily focused on continuous improvement, we reject the idea that quality means 'getting it right the first time' or 'zero defects'. Mistakes are OK; they are to be expected. But they must be a source of a new learning experience and of progress.

We envisage four levels at which development must occur and which must share at least some common unifying goal if quality enhancement is to be likely. At each level, to a differing degree, there must be understanding of student learning and of the conditions which encourage high quality learning.

The levels of development, while separated for the purposes of exposition, overlap and intermesh so that progress in one affects all the others.

First level: *Individual development: students, teachers and mentors* – improvement of students' learning experience by lecturers who are trained in university teaching methods and, we hope, are developing as 'reflective practitioners' in partnership with colleagues (mainly but not exclusively departmentally-based).

Second level: *Departmental and course team development: networking and review* – improvement of the immediate environment for students, ie, course or departmental development.

Third level: *Institutional development: change agency, resistance and policy integration* – improvement of the 'remote' environment for students and lecturers, ie, organizational development, provision of appropriate facilities and opportunities to assist departments and individuals.

Fourth level: *Development at the national level* – improvement of the national infrastructure for quality enhancement, including the need for more widespread dissemination of good practice arising from various funding and research initiatives and identification of excellence during quality reviews.

Individual development: students, teachers and mentors

When we spoke about the matter of improving students' learning experience in Chapter 4 we signalled a number of key characteristics of high quality learning and the necessary but not sufficient conditions under which high quality learning occurs. In painting such a picture we also offered suggestions for developing a high quality learning environment, where interdependency, active and deep learning, promoting responsibility in learning on the part of students, using student experience as a learning resource and so on, are an integral feature of a *higher* education.

In our reading of the literature and from our own and others' practice, we described in Chapter 5 a number of principles which may be used to good effect for developing the thinking and action of students, of teachers as curriculum designers and deliverers, and of institutional managers. We are well aware, too, that some individuals within institutions have attempted to put into practice some if not all of these ideas but they frequently suffer innovation isolation. The present climate in higher education, certainly in the UK and Australia, is changing rapidly, however, in that institutions need to disseminate and build on the isolated examples of good practice that undoubtedly exist through policy-led initiatives and a corporate vision emanating from the most senior academics and university leaders. Mechanisms for the process of drawing together include 'quality circles', loose 'networks' of practitioners and formal 'action enquiry networks' as described below at the level of 'Departmental and course team development'.

A further matter at the first level of development relates to the training of university lecturers in teaching and learning. We strongly advocate that new lecturers receive such training as a first step in improving the quality of university education. The case studies offer examples of such training programmes in action. Minimally, such training courses (centrally provided by educational development units) should aim to enhance teaching in universities as a career through focusing on the professional development needs of lecturers by:

■ developing flexible teaching and tutoring styles;
■ encouraging flexible approaches to course design and development;
■ raising awareness of student characteristics and learning processes;
■ enhancing competencies fundamental to carrying out the teaching role:
    – in large as well as in small groups,
    – in different instructional settings (eg, classrooms/labs/field work/ practicals),
    – in assessing student progress, and
    – in evaluating courses and teaching;
■ laying the foundations for continuing professional development.

In addition, we recommend that lecturers undergoing training should be closely supported in their induction period by mentors from their discipline who, in turn, are also trained for this specialized and demanding task. Working with a mentor and with a group of 'critical friends' is particularly valuable, we feel, as a means for individuals and course teams to create an ethos of quality enhancement. Mentoring has the added value of creating a skilled group of staff with expertise in:

■ operating as a reflective practitioner in relation to improving one's own and others' teaching, by
    – collaborating with colleagues in investigating how best to teach their own subject,
    – operating as a member of a community of enquirers into the improvement of the theory and practice of teaching;
■ mentorship and acting as an internal consultant in teaching and learning, which might include *inter alia*
    – acting as a counsellor in matters concerned with the teaching of adults,
    – observing and appraising teaching, including ways of providing observational and other feedback to junior colleagues that is sensitive, appropriate and constructive,
    – identifying the strengths and weaknesses of new lecturers with a view to helping them to develop, implement and evaluate personal action plans geared to the improvement of their teaching performance.

Moreover, mentoring serves a very important role in the life of an academic department and particularly for course teams through the cultivation of an ethos of critical friendship. We have used the idea of a group of critical friends in networking and action research on many university courses and with university academic staff. The idea is that peers give support and feedback to colleagues about the progress of their enquiries in teaching by providing a critique of actions undertaken and planned.

In order to operate effectively in working this way with staff and students at a variety of levels, our experience tells us that discussion is most successful when it is conducted within a framework of relationships characterized by mutual trust, openness, honesty, respect for persons, sensitivity, positive and constructive forms of expression and a commitment to the success of others' inquiry as well as one's own. Members of critical friends' groups have a role to assist each other in the development of these qualities, helping to promote the skills of being an active listener, providing clear descriptions, giving affirmation and encouragement yet also tactfully offering alternative ideas in constructive rather than negative criticism.

The qualities cultivated by critical friends' groups, then, are ones which contribute to good professional *dialogue* (cf. Senge, 1990) not only in the context of an immediate quality project, but also in other professional settings. Transfer to other settings with other focuses is our intention, and the outcome is lifelong and collaborative learning. In this way, Senge believes a 'learning organization' is formed through the creative cut-and-thrust of dialogue and discussion across and within departments and course teams. This leads us into an overview of the next level of development.

Departmental and course team development: networking and review

At the second level in developing quality in organizations the question of how course teams or departments may improve their practice in terms of quality enhancement arises. We offer a number of practical steps that departments could take in becoming more effective as locations where student and staff learning about learning and teaching methods and quality improvement occurs – in short, where dialogue about appropriate systems for supporting the main business of universities (teaching and research) takes place.

We believe that interacting agents are necessary for achieving quality enhancement (see Chapter 3) and it is in this sense that course or departmental teams need to 'pull together' in ways that hitherto may not have pervaded departmental life as strongly as they could or should have. Two ways that this feature of corporate life has been described in the literature on organizational development are quality circles and networks.

Both are driven by the need to share ideas and experiences so that, for instance, wheels are not reinvented and a spirit of camaraderie is established. In an important sense, 'pulling together' through team work has been at the heart of effective organizations outside of the academic community (Senge, 1990). Indeed, networking is now being used as a vehicle for improving teaching and staff development in higher education (see O'Neil, 1991, 1993). The central issues may be unpacked by reference to the notion of networking as a process for developing and refining professional dialogue with a view to improving practice. Three main types of professional communication relevant to networking can then be identified:

- *professional dialogue* which is characterized by the infrequent and random transfer of ideas and experience among colleagues;
- *practitioner networks* in which colleagues agree to cooperate in a systematic way to share insights; and
- *action enquiry networks* in which university teachers come together as a team with the aim of developing their practical knowledge.

Networking means strengthening the links that already exist among colleagues and, indeed, extending the net by actively seeking to incorporate others. This will mean increasing interdependent communications among university teachers with a view to disseminating ideas about current teaching and learning practice through action and critique.

In non-networked systems, this type of collaboration lacks coherence and structure. As a result, knowledge loss is common and knowledge transfer random. For networks to operate effectively, then, there needs to be agreement among participants on an appropriate system for the regular exchange of information. This feature of networks distinguishes them from casual meetings of staff at educational development seminars and workshops where any one person's attendance is erratic and group membership fluid. Non-networked systems of communication operate on the principle of interaction 'as the spirit moves you'.

Checking out the information supplied in a systematic way to evaluate experience results in the notion of 'action networks'. Such uses of information to improve decision making and action mean that gaps in know-how among, say, teaching team members are significantly reduced, for in networked professional communications there are agreed procedures for reflection, action and the free flow of information (see Chapter 6). In a networked action enquiry system, the presence of these factors necessarily brings about a 'qualitative change in the practice of participants' (Bell and Pennington, 1989, p.66).

To recapitulate, *networks and action research* (see Bell and Pennington, 1989; O'Neil, 1990) are interrelated approaches to improve professional dialogue involving a commitment on the part of all participants to exchange ideas and experience, to disseminate widely the outcomes of these exchanges and to engage in critical reflection on their practice with a view to its improvement. For a network to operate successfully, then, a course team needs to work systematically on problems that they have identified in order to produce realistic solutions and action plans that are implemented and evaluated to assess actual as opposed to predicted results.

Four key problems in implementing any development initiative aimed at enhancing the quality of university teaching and learning may be identified, namely:

- *getting started* in those universities which have not yet formally adopted quality enhancement initiatives;
- *using existing information and techniques to enlighten decision making* in universities already developing and about to launch quality initiatives on teaching and learning;
- *facilitating action learning* on the part of all participants in the quality enhancement processes in universities on teaching and learning (see Chapter 6); and
- *sharing practical knowledge and evaluated experience* with the whole of the 'community of quality' within and without the organization.

The concept of networking has been introduced to indicate its potential for modifying and improving existing channels of professional communication and, at the same time, for addressing quality enhancement in teaching and learning. A key factor in this endeavour to improve information flow will be the identification and involvement of link agents. This means, minimally, identifying learning agents to facilitate information networks.

In an extended action network sense, it will also mean participating with a view to improving practice. Staff will therefore need to be developed as *change agents* as well as *link agents*. Networking is a powerful strategy to improve dialogue among colleagues about ways and means of enhancing the quality of teaching and learning. It should be extended past the departmental level to the institutional and national level into the 'shadow networks' which Schön (1971) pictures filling the gaps between various elements within complex systems such as higher education (see pp.39–40).

Critical self-review and self-evaluation are further requirements for departmental and course team effectiveness (see Adelman and Alexander, 1982; McDonald and Roe, 1984). We have been suggesting that at every stage the *key question* must be asked: 'How does whatever we are doing or proposing to do contribute to achieving the primary goal of higher education and/or high quality learning outcomes and/or the conditions which will make that achievement possible?' Such a question will, we hope, be a core concern for departments in their efforts to secure the highest quality of provision. But self-evaluating *departments* will, at a minimum, also attend to the sorts of questions posed in the following list:

- appropriateness and quality of courses: curricula, teaching methods and facilities for helping students to learn how to learn;
- appropriateness and quality of research and staff development to underpin quality in teaching-learning;
- whether accommodation, facilities, resource deployment, administrative processes and support structures are serving the department and its students adequately;
- whether there is adequate liaison and communication between this department and cognate departments, the rest of the institution and relevant outside bodies;
- what are the perceived strengths of this department and how may they be cultivated for the common good, and what are the weaknesses and how may they be put right?

Clearly, the data flowing from such a critical self review will inform decisions taken in determining the strategic direction(s) the department will follow in achieving high quality learning and teaching. Moreover, such evaluations will reveal departmental priorities for short- and long-term action and be a source of information for reflecting on progress towards policy goals.

Matters of interest to specific *course teams* in the quality improvement undertaking are many, but the following checklist is offered as a starting point:

- what are the goals and philosophy of the course team in relation to quality improvement?
- how will the teaching team create the conditions necessary for high quality learning to occur (see Chapter 4)?
- to what extent is the course team pursuing an active policy for staff development and curriculum renewal? What is the policy?
- how are members of the teaching team sharing their problems and successes through peer support groups or networks?
- what means are the course team using to induct new team members?
- how will the course leader know that he or she has an effective operation? How are learning outcomes assessed (see Chapter 8)?
- what innovations to overcome resource constraints have been implemented?
- is research and development in teaching and learning an accepted routine feature of the day-to-day activities of teachers (individually and collectively) on this course?

- how do the key players (staff, students, employers, graduates, etc.) regard (value) this course?

Institutional development: change agency, resistance and policy integration

At the institutional level, too, the key question about impact on learning and on the conditions to foster it must be asked repeatedly. It may well be that it is an individual acting as a change agent who keeps pressing that question, or the agent may be a group or even a whole organization which not only learns from reflection on action but also constructively addresses the current instability in organizations and in systems such as higher education. The networks discussed above are necessary at this level as well to disseminate that learning and the action which results from it.

What does it take to be a change agent or to belong to a group which will foster change? Basically, a large dose of optimism and a passionate commitment to improving the system in whatever way one can. We meet people with that commitment to higher education daily and we are suggesting that we may become more effective change agents together if we agree to articulate at least a similar perspective on quality in higher education. Moreover, Entwistle's (1992) review of the literature on the effect of different teaching and assessment methods on student learning outcomes proves that there is a body of knowledge which must be assimilated by those who would improve the quality of teaching and learning. It should not be too hard to get agreement on the following principles:

- Effectiveness can be improved at every level of the higher education system.
- Critical reflection and action learning are highly effective strategies for enhancing quality in most spheres but are especially appropriate to higher education.
- We must not lose sight of the primary purpose of higher education and we must not allow our energies to be misdirected to activities which do not directly contribute to achieving it. (We hope we have found a form of words which is acceptable to many of our colleagues to state that purpose succinctly.)
- We must plan our teaching with high quality learning outcomes in mind and we must be able to demonstrate that our students achieve those outcomes.
- We must accept our responsibilities for helping students achieve quality learning outcomes but we must also hold others accountable for their responsibilities – especially students and funding bodies.

If we share those principles, the consequences for our actions will be that each of us:

- encourages others to make high quality learning the chief priority in planning, development and review activities;
- advocates the use of action learning strategies to address problems at all levels of the organization;
- aids and abets the formation of networks of people who will share ideas and good practice and support each other's efforts;
- calls for reforms to organizational structures and institutional practice which will contribute to achieving the goal of high quality learning;
- encourages others – students, academics, external stakeholders – to learn about learning so as to make sensible efforts to enhance its quality.

We will probably be known as nuisances, but we will be persistent and articulate and we will be consistent. It will probably mean getting into trouble. We must be extremely knowledgeable advocates and we must practice what we preach.

In short, we are suggesting that each of us in the system carries some responsibility for development at all levels and that we can make a difference. In Chapter 7 we canvassed the reasons that it is so difficult to create 'learning organizations' and some of the strategies for overcoming those difficulties. If one were in a position to institute or help implement a major change programme, one would need to take account of the following *causes of resistance*. These have been identified by Pennington (1989) who, in reflecting on the introduction of the Enterprise in Higher Education Initiative, generates a number of propositions (pp.11–12) representing the 'practical wisdom of development'.

- Change is good for *other* people.

A widespread recognition that quality is important and that change is needed does not necessarily imply that staff will cooperate in practice. Those managing quality improvement programmes will, therefore, need to determine who the 'critical mass' of supporters are and work through and with them. Crudely, this means working with the 'healthy' parts of an organization first: that is, with those who are committed to an innovation and are prepared to help themselves and others.

- Academic staff will tend to resist all forms of change which leave them with less control over their own courses and students.

Academics are defensive of their own autonomy and authority in all that they do, but their 'territorial imperative' is probably strongest in what they choose to teach and how they teach it. For a project involving a substantial change in approach to teaching and learning, this means being alert to any implications that would undermine the control and independence of academic staff in course design and delivery. Indeed, there is a constant need to monitor proposed and actual changes so as to guarantee the continuing independence of action on the part of all participants.

- Resistance to change is proportional to the force driving an innovation. The larger the push, the larger the resistance.

This means that the initiators of quality programmes need to think as much about reducing resistance to their scheme as to its advocacy and dissemination. Or it may mean consciously starting small and nurturing a project so it spreads to other areas, or draws others in (for example, see O'Neil, 1991).

- Where there is a constant and high demand for change some individuals feel threatened and react defensively – often by using former practices more secretly or by modifying new practices in such a way that they increasingly resemble the old.

In such cases, quality project managers should be cautious of superficial movement said to represent a fundamental change. 'Critical friendship' and collaboration with colleagues on teaching and learning enhancement projects might just nudge forward the process of innovating in a way that is less threatening. Of course, an issue here is that of the 'ownership' of the innovation and without ownership there is seldom commitment.

- Nostalgia for a mythical past of fixed hopes, aims and ambitions when staff were settled, respected and knew where they were going is just that – nostalgia.

Consequently, quality projects must identify and engage with participants' personal theories and practices and recognize the potent influence that such ideas and beliefs have on behaviour. In addition, quality programmes must address the fact that change is an enduring feature of academic life as we move into the twenty-first century – the canoeing metaphor of 'permanent white water' is an apposite slogan for all participants in quality improvement activities.

- If individuals have little confidence in their own abilities they are less willing to try out alternative approaches to course delivery.

Any self-improvement project, therefore, needs to examine ways of boosting the self-esteem of all participants so that they are capable of giving and receiving feedback about their own and others' teaching. 'People cannot be developed. They can only develop themselves'. (Julius Nyerere, 1973)

- Tired, hard-pressed or harangued staff don't innovate because change often involves a deal of conflict, bother and hard work.

Academic life over the past five to ten years has moved at a frenetic pace: new courses have been introduced with new structures and with more students, indeed with a larger variety of students. 'Efficiency gains' demanded by governments have been met, though in many instances these have translated into 'more for less' on the ground. In this context, it is hardly surprising that staff are jaded through overwork and to some extent dispirited by the apparently never-ending succession of squeezes on resources. Academic managers should heed one clear imperative: in managing change programmes, seek ways of reducing staff workloads before adding new work.

In some institutions there may be such opportunities for coordinated large scale programmes of change, but we have been suggesting throughout this book that where this is too ambitious, a ripple effect strategy is worth trying. No attempt to improve the quality of learning is too small; most can have wider impact (through those vital networks and groupings of critical friends); and most can draw in others who will learn about learning from the experience of working even on a small-scale project. In addition, we can encourage and support the type of human resource management strategies Pennington lists at the end of his case study (Chapter 3) to help create a climate in which such efforts are valued. Furthermore, in devising a workable strategy for teaching and learning at an organizational level, we believe that it is necessary for universities to:

- align strategic objectives in teaching and learning with those of their institution as a whole – for example, to show tangibly how commitment to 'scholarship and research', 'access', 'flexibility', 'internationalism', 'equity', and all those similar 'vision' statements carry over into *students' actual experience of the curriculum*;
- acknowledge what is known about effective learning from recent research and good professional practice by ensuring that this underpins students' learning experiences through the *appropriate design of new courses and the updating of existing ones*;
- acknowledge the prior learning experiences of students, many of whom have already been exposed to curricula which incorporate the acquisition of personal and social transferable skills, student-centred approaches to teaching, the development of capability/competences/outcomes and self-regulated learning, not only as at present in appropriate credit accumulation and transfers systems but also in *curriculum design and delivery processes*;
- ensure that students, irrespective of module choice, programme of study or degree route, experience a *high quality learning experience* during their time at university;

- recognize that changes in approaches to teaching and learning on a broad institutional front will only be effective when *integrated with appropriate policies, strategies and resources for staff development, curriculum renewal, quality assurance, information technology, learning support and the physical learning environment.*

Few universities are presently at a stage in their evolution where functional integration occurs among these iterative strategies.

In this strategic and operational endeavour, all stakeholders may find the six general questions used by quality auditors in the UK (Gordon, 1993) of assistance in developing a community of quality, namely:

- what are you trying to do?
- why are you trying to do it?
- how are you doing it?
- why are you doing it that way?
- why do you think that is the best way of doing it?
- how do you know it works?

Development at the national level

With our more focused description of what constitutes high quality learning and how to encourage it, we are in a much better position to analyse the likely impacts of various initiatives of our governments to ensure quality and accountability in higher education. As we have seen from our case studies, the impact of these initiatives has not been entirely negative. In fact, some very positive efforts have been made in most institutions to respond to these challenges. In addition, a significant number of national initiatives have been launched both in Britain and in Australia (eg, Committee for the Advancement of University Teaching and Enterprise in Higher Education).

The trouble is they appear piecemeal. It almost goes without saying that some form of 'pulling together' is required through a national agency where insights are collected and then disseminated for the good of the combined endeavour. But problems arise here, too. Quality agencies themselves seem, in the UK especially, to have grown dramatically in number over the past three to four years. In relation to teaching and learning, for instance, in Britain there are:

- separate funding agencies for England, Wales and Scotland, each with a quality assessment unit uniquely its own;
- discrete bodies for quality audit (one UK-wide agency) and assessment – when previously under the CNAA, for example, these functions were integrated;

■ significant overlaps in the quality enhancement function through the HEQC/Quality Enhancement Division and the CVCP/Universities' Staff Development Unit, setting aside the various informal professional bodies such as the Staff and Educational Development Association (offering, for instance, a national accreditation scheme for the initial training of lecturers).

How is all of this to be coordinated? Moreover, apart from the actual and opportunity cost to the higher education system of such a duplication of effort, we could pose an awkward question or two about the real impact or effectiveness of these inspectorial agencies in making a worthwhile contribution to quality enhancement of teaching and learning and to the overarching purpose of higher education.

Bridging the gap between the audit and assessment of quality (at a systems or even a classroom level) and its enhancement (at the level of teaching and learning) is another significant national problem that seems to us to have received little attention from policy-makers. How, for instance, is peer observation of classroom teaching, required in the UK as an element in quality assessment, to work? What training programme do assessors really need if the assessed teachers are to feel confident that a thorough professional job has been done? (We note with concern the two day duration of the training workshop that they currently undergo!) What are the assessors observing, in any case, when they make judgements? Is this more to do with their own preference for a specific mode or model of teaching and if so what is this? Or is it more to do with what we claim quality teaching and learning is about? 'Who assesses the assessors?' is, after all, not a hollow question when millions of dollars are at stake, as in the 1993–4 Australian round of 'quality awards' where the explicit intention of government is that only 50 per cent of universities will be 'rewarded'. A key matter, of course, is whether or not they could ever be impartial or neutral in such a politically-charged context. If the 1991 UK White Paper is to be believed, then the future matter of differential funding of teaching will leave some institutions wondering whether some assessors have axes to grind, let alone prejudices to air.

At another level of debate, we continue to be disturbed by certain unintended outcomes of the quality initiatives in Australia and the United Kingdom. Foremost among these is the very negative impact of competition for funds – whether they are offered as a reward on top of base funding as in Australia or whether rank order in a quality assessment determines whether a department gets research money at all as in the UK. Already we have each experienced others not wishing to collaborate on major projects when the kudos (and money) would have to be shared, or withholding documents from which others might get good ideas, or not wanting to talk about planned or on-going research or development strategies for fear of not getting credit for being the innovator. This is a new, very unwelcome and ultimately counter-productive experience.

In addition, there is the constant pressure to respond to more and more demands for data and information, to prepare quality portfolios or receive audit teams, to bid for funds from various government departments, research councils and other bodies. We understand only too clearly the desperation of our students who complain that all their essays are due at once and they never get time to learn anything!

It is harder to be heard outside the walls of one's own institution, but just as persistence and consistency and a clearly articulated position coupled with a strategy for promoting learning about learning can gradually have an effect internally, we believe that the ripples can spread further. For instance, steering committees for externally-funded projects may include very influential people who may come to share some of our priorities and understandings by working with us, or course review teams may recruit those they wish to influence to assist with evaluations or curriculum development. We do not see this as a cynical, political exercise but as an important opportunity to include other stakeholders in our learning community for our mutual benefit; we are going to learn from them, too. That is the nature of action learning.

Conclusion

We cannot claim to have solved the problem of achieving quality learning in higher education, but we hope we have managed to help a few readers make it outside the maze of trees to a point where the forest becomes visible once again. For what it is worth, we have found ourselves asking the big question every now and then: 'How does this proposal contribute to the achievement of a learning environment where students will learn to form and substantiate independent thought and action in a coherent and articulate fashion?', and once in a while it leads to a reconsideration of an idea which seemed plausible until its benefits were carefully considered. If only more of the stakeholders throughout the system of higher education would try to learn about learning and how to encourage it, we believe there would be much less pressure for accountability and much more quality.

References

Abbott, J and Lonsdale, A (1992) *Academic Staff Appraisal and Performance Management: the Australian experience*, Geelong, Vic: Deakin University Press.

Adelman, C and Alexander, RJ (1982) *The Self Evaluating Institution*, London: Methuen.

Allen, M (1988) *The Goals of Universities*, Milton Keynes: SRHE/Open University Press.

Andresen, LW (1991) 'Introduction to university teaching: issues in course design', in Ross, B (ed.) *Research and Development in Higher Education 13: Teaching for effective learning*, Sydney: HERDSA, pp.45–52.

Andresen, L, Nightingale, P, Boud, D and Magin, D (1992) *Strategies for Assessing Students*, Teaching with Reduced Resources Series, Sydney: Professional Development Centre, University of New South Wales.

Argyris, C (1982) *Reasoning, Learning and Action: Individual and organizational*, San Francisco, CA: Jossey-Bass.

Argyris, C (1990) *Overcoming Organizational Defenses: Facilitating organizational learning*, Boston, Mass: Allyn and Bacon.

Argyris, C (1991) 'Teaching smart people how to learn', *Harvard Business Review*, 69, 3, 99–109.

Argyris, C and Schön, D (1974) *Theory in Practice: Increasing professional effectiveness*, San Francisco, CA: Jossey-Bass.

Argyris, C and Schön, D (1978) *Organizational Learning: A theory of action perspective*, Reading, Mass: Addison-Wesley.

Argyris, C and Schön, D (1989) 'Participatory action research and action science compared: a commentary', *American Behavioral Scientist*, 32, 5, 612–23.

Badley, G (1992) 'Institutional values and teaching quality', in Barnett, R (ed.) *Learning to Effect*, Buckingham: Society for Research into Higher Education and Open University Press.

Baldwin, P (1991) *Higher Education: Quality and Diversity in the 1990s*, policy statement by the Minister for Higher Education and Employment Services. Canberra: Australian Government Publishing Service.

Barnett, R (1990) *The Idea of Higher Education*, Buckingham: Open University Press.

Barnett, R (1992a) *Improving Higher Education: Total quality care*, Buckingham: Society for Research into Higher Education and Open University Press.

Barnett, R (ed.) (1992b) *Learning to Effect*, Buckingham: Society for Research into Higher Education and Open University Press.

Becher, T (1989) *Academic Tribes and Territories*, Buckingham: Open University Press.

Beckhard, R (1990) 'Strategies for large system change', in Kolb, D, Rubin, I and Osland, J (eds) *Organizational Behavior: Practical readings for managers*, Englewood Cliffs, NJ: Prentice-Hall.

Bell, GH (1988) 'Using action inquiry', in Nias, J and Groundwater-Smith, S (eds) *The Enquiring Teacher: Supporting and sustaining teacher research*, London: Falmer Press.

Bell, GH and Pennington, RC (1989) *Action Learning and School Focused Study*, Sheffield: Manpower Services Commission and Sheffield City Polytechnic.

Biggs, JB (1987) *Student Approaches to Learning and Studying*, Hawthorn, Vic: Australian Council for Educational Research.

Biggs, JB (1989) 'Does learning about learning help teachers with teaching? Psychology and the tertiary teacher', inaugural lecture, 8 December 1988, *Supplement to the Gazette*, University of Hong Kong, XXXVI, 1, 20 March 1989.

Biggs, JB (1991) 'Student learning in the context of school', in Biggs, JB (ed.) *Teaching for Learning: The view from cognitive psychology*, Hawthorn, Vic: Australian Council for Educational Research, pp. 7–29.

Biggs, JB and Collis, KF (1982) *Evaluating the Quality of Learning: The SOLO taxonomy*, New York: Academic Press.

Biggs, JB and Moore, PJ (1992) *The Process of Learning* (3rd edn), Sydney: Prentice-Hall.

Boud, D (ed.) (1985a) *Problem-Based Learning in Education for the Professions*, Sydney: Higher Education Research and Development Society of Australasia.

Boud, D, Keogh, R and Walker, D (eds) (1985b) *Reflection: Turning experience into learning*, London: Kogan Page.

Boud, D and Felletti, G (eds) (1991) *The Challenge of Problem-Based Learning*, London: Kogan Page.

Brown, S, Jones, G and Rawnsley, S (1993) *Observing Teaching*, SCED Paper 79, Birmingham: Standing Conference on Educational Development.

Brown, H and Sommerlad, E (1992) 'Staff development in higher education – towards the learning organisation?', *Higher Education Quarterly*, 46, 2, 174–90.

Carr, W and Kemmis, S (1986) *Becoming Critical: Education, knowledge and action research*, London: Falmer Press.

Chippendale, P and Collins, C (1991) *Values, Ethics, and the Nature of Social Reality*, Brisbane: Zygon Publishers for the Australian Values Institute.

Clare, CP (1993) 'A strategic planning system for a new university', MBA dissertation, Warwick University.

Clark, B (1983) *The Higher Education System: Academic organization in a cross-national perspective*, London: University of California Press.

Clarke, JA and Taylor, PG (1993) 'An overview of the Teaching and Learning in Tertiary Education Project', paper delivered at the 5th European Conference of EARLI, Aix en Provence, 31 August to 5 September 1993.

Clayton, M (1993) 'Towards total quality management in higher education: Aston University – a case study', *Higher Education*, 25, 3, 363–72.

Coate, E (1993) 'The introduction of total quality management at Oregon State University', *Higher Education*, 25, 3, 303–20.

Cole, JR (1993) 'Balancing acts' in *Daedalus*, 122, 4, The American Research University.

Colling, C (1993) 'Teaching quality revisited: Warnock words for policy practice', *Quality Assurance in Higher Education*, 1, 3, 21–5.

Committee of Directors of Polytechnics (1992) 'Higher education: Quality and change. Developments toward a new system', briefing paper.

Cornesky, R and McCool, S (1992) *Total Quality Improvement Guide for Institutions of Higher Education*, Madison, WI: Magna Publications.

Cornesky, R *et al.* (1990) *Using Deming to Improve Quality in Colleges and Universities*, Madison, WI: Magna Publications.

Cornesky, R, McCool, S, Byrnes, L and Weber, R (1991) *Implementing Total Quality Management in Higher Education*, Madison, WI: Magna Publications.

Crosby, PB (1989) *Let's Talk Quality*, New York: McGraw-Hill.

Dalton, G (1984) 'Influence and organizational change', in Kolb, D, Rubin, I and McIntyre, J (eds) *Organizational Psychology*, Englewood Cliffs, NJ: Prentice-Hall.

Dawkins, J (1988) *Higher Education: A policy statement*, Canberra: Australian Government Publishing Service.

Day, C (1993) 'Reflection: a necessary but not sufficient condition for professional development', *British Educational Research Journal*, 19, 83–93.

Deming, W (1986) *Out of the Crisis*, Cambridge, MA: MIT Press.

Department of Education and Science (1985) *The Development of Higher Education into the 1990s*, London: HMSO.

Department of Education and Science (1987) *Higher Education: Meeting the challenge*, London: HMSO.

Department of Education and Science (1991) *Higher Education: A new framework*, London: HMSO.

DfE (1993) *The Charter for Higher Education*, London: Department for Education.

Dick, B (1991) *Helping Groups To Be Effective*, (2nd edn), Brisbane: Interchange.

Doherty, G (1993) 'Towards total quality management in higher education: a case study of the University of Wolverhampton', *Higher Education*, 25, 3, 321–40.

Doyle, W and Ponder, G (1977–8) 'The practicality ethic in teacher decision-making', *Interchange*, 8, 3, 1–12.

Doyle, W, Sanford, J and Emmer, E (1983) *Managing Academic Tasks in Junior High School: Background, design, methodology*, (Report No 6185), Austin: University of Texas, Research and Development Centre for Teacher Education.

Duke, C (1992) *The Learning University: Towards a new paradigm?*, Buckingham: Society for Research in Higher Education and Open University Press.

Dunlap, L (1990) 'Language and power: teaching writing to third world graduate students', in Sanyal, B (ed.) *Breaking the Boundaries: A one-world approach to planning education*, New York: Plenum Press.

Ellis, R (1993a) 'The management of quality in the University of Ulster', *Higher Education*, 25, 3, 239–58.

Ellis, R (ed.) (1993b) *Quality Assurance for University Teaching*, Buckingham: Society for Research into Higher Education and Open University Press.

Elton, L (1993) 'University teaching: a professional model for quality', in Ellis, R (ed.) *Quality Assurance for University Teaching*, Buckingham: Society for Research into Higher Education and Open University Press, pp.133–46.

Elton, L and Partington, P (1991) *Teaching Standards and Excellence in Higher Education: Developing a culture for quality*, London: Committee of Vice-Chancellors and Principals.

Entwistle, N (1992) *The Impact of Teaching on Learning Outcomes in Higher Education: A literature review*, Sheffield: Committee of Vice-Chancellors and Principals/ Universities' Staff Development Unit.

Freire, P and Shor, I (1987) *A Pedagogy for Liberation*, Basingstoke: Macmillan.

Fuller, T (1989) *The Voice of Liberal Learning*, London: Yale.

Geddes, T (1993a) 'The total quality initiative at South Bank University', *Higher Education*, 25, 3, 341–62.

Geddes, T (1993b) *Total Quality Management*, London: South Bank University.

Gibbs, G (1992a) *Improving the Quality of Student Learning*, Bristol: Technical and Education Services.

Gibbs, G (1992b) 'Improving the quality of student learning through course design', in Barnett, R (ed.), *Learning to Effect*, Buckingham: Society for Research into Higher Education and Open University Press.

Gibbs, G (1992c) *Teaching More Students*, vols 1–5, London: Polytechnics and Colleges Funding Council.

Gibbs, G and Habeshaw, T (1989) *Preparing to Teach: An introduction to effective teaching in higher education*, Bristol: Technical and Educational Services.

Glaser, BG and Strauss, AL (1967) *The Discovery of Grounded Theory*, Chicago, IL: Aldine.

Gordon, G (1993) 'The audit and assessment of teaching quality: an auditor's view', in Knight, PT (ed.) *The Audit and Assessment of Teaching Quality*, Birmingham: Standing Conference on Educational Development and SRHE.

Gore, EW (1993) 'Total quality management in education', in Hibberd, DL (ed.) *Continuous Quality Improvement*, Maryville: Prescott Publishing.

Grundy, S (1986) *Curriculum Quality Improvement*, Maryville: Prescott Publishing.

Guskey, TR (1986) 'Staff development and the process of teacher change', *Educational Researcher*, 15, 5, 5–12.

Habermas, J (1978) *Knowledge and Human Interests*, London: Heinemann.

Hanks, P (ed.) (1979) *Collins Dictionary of the English Language*, Sydney: Collins.

Hansen, W (1993) 'Bringing total quality improvement into the college classroom', *Higher Education*, 25, 3, 259–80.

Harrison, R (1993) 'Using portfolios for personal and career development', in Assiter, A and Shaw, E (eds) *Using Records of Achievement in Higher Education*, London: Kogan Page.

Harvey, L, Burrows, A and Green, D (1992) *Criteria of Quality: Summary paper*, Birmingham: Quality in Higher Education Project, University of Central England in Birmingham.

Hativa, N and Raviv, A (1993) 'Using a single score for summative teacher evaluation by students', *Research in Higher Education*, 35; 625–46.

Hau, I (1992) 'Teaching quality improvement by quality improvement in teaching', Report No 59, Madison, WI: Centre for Quality and Productivity Improvement, University of Wisconsin.

Hibberd, DL (ed.) (1993) *Continuous Quality Improvement*, Maryville: Prescott Publishing.

Higher Education (1993) 25, 3, special issue on TQM in higher education.

Higher Education Council (1990) *Higher Education: The challenges ahead*, Canberra: Australian Government Publishing Service.

Higher Education Council (1992a) *The Quality of Higher Education: Discussion Papers*, Canberra: Australian Government Publishing Service.

Higher Education Council (1992b) *The Quality of Higher Education: Draft advice*, Canberra: Australian Government Publishing Service.

Higher Education Council (1992c) *Achieving Quality*, Canberra: Australian Government Publishing Service.

Hughes, C and Sohler, C (1992) 'Can performance management work in Australian universities?', *Higher Education*, 24, 1, 41–56.

Imai, M (1986) *Kaizen: The Key to Japan's Competitive Success*, New York: Random House.

Juran, JM (1988) *Juran on Planning for Quality*, New York: Free Press.

Kagan, DM (1992) 'Implications of research on teacher belief', *Educational Psychologist*, 27, 65–90.

Kemmis, S (1988) *The Action Research Reader* (3rd edn), Victoria: Deakin University.

Knowles, M (1978) *The Adult Learner: A neglected species*, Houston, TX: Gulf Publishing Company.

Kolb, D and Frohman, A (1970) 'An organization development approach to consulting', *Sloan Management Review*, 12, 51–65.

Kolb, D, Rubin, I and Osland, J (1991) *Organizational Behavior: An experiential approach*, (5th edn), Englewood Cliffs, NJ: Prentice-Hall.

Lewin, K (1947) 'Frontiers in group dynamics', *Human Relations*, 1, 5–41.

Lewin, K (1952) 'Group decisions and social change', in Swanson, G, Newcomb, T and Hartley, F (eds) *Readings in Social Psychology*, New York: Holt.

Lieberman, A (ed.) (1986) *Building a Professional Culture in Schools*, New York: Teachers College Press.

Limerick, D (1993) 'The shape of the new organisation: implications for universities', unpublished conference paper, Australian Institute of Tertiary Education Administrators.

Liverpool John Moores University (1993) *Student Charter*, Liverpool: John Moores University.

Lockwood, G and Davies, J (1985) *Universities: The management challenge*, Windsor: SRHE and NFER-Nelson.

McDonald, R and Roe, E (1984) *Reviewing Departments*, HERDSA Green Guide No.1, Sydney: Higher Education Research and Development Society of Australasia.

McFarlane, A (1992). *Teaching and Learning in an Expanding Higher Education System*, report of the working party of the Committee of Scottish University Principals.

Macnair, G (1990) 'The British Enterprise in Higher Education Initiative', *Higher Education Management*, 2, 1, 60–71.

Marton, F (1981) 'Phenomenography – describing conceptions of the world around us', *Instructional Science*, 10, 177–200.

Marton, F, Dall'Alba, G and Beaty, E (1992) 'Conceptions of Learning', *International Journal of Educational Research*, 46, 81–104.

Marton, F, Hounsell, D and Entwistle, N (eds) (1984) *The Experience of Learning*, Edinburgh: Scottish Academic Press.

Middlehurst, R (1992) 'Quality: an organising principle for higher education?', *Higher Education Quarterly*, 46, 1, 20–38.

Miller, RL and Cangemi, JP (1993) 'Why total quality management fails: perspective of top management', *Journal of Management Development*, 12, 7, 40–50.

Mink, O (1991) '"We are not in Kansas anymore, Toto": creating new organisational paradigms for change', *Total Quality Management Institute 1991 Conference Proceedings*, Melbourne: TQMI.

Mink, O, Schultz, J and Mink, B (1991) *Open Organisations* (2nd edn), Austin, TX: Catapult Press.

Morgan, A (1993) *Improving Your Students' Learning: Reflections on the experience of study*, London: Kogan Page.

Nadler, D (1987) 'The effective management of organizational change', in Lorsch, J (ed.) *Handbook of Organizational Behavior*, New York: Prentice-Hall, pp.358–69.

National Union of Students (1992) *NUS Student Charter*, London: NUS.

Nyerere, J (1973) *Freedom and Development*, Dar es Salaam: Oxford University Press.

O'Neil, MJ (1990) *Networks and Networking for the Professional Development of Staff in African Universities*, report prepared for The British Council, London.

O'Neil, MJ (1991) 'Networking: from candlepower through floodlighting to daylight', in Gibbs, G (ed.) *31 Ideas for Staff and Educational Development*, SCED paper No. 61, Birmingham Polytechnic.

O'Neil, M and Pennington, G (1992) *Evaluating Teaching and Courses from an Active Learning Perspective*, module 12 of Effective Learning and Teaching in Higher Education Series, Sheffield: CVCP/Universities' Staff Development and Training Unit.

O'Neil, M J (1993) *Improving Practice and Enhancing Quality in University Teaching and Learning in Ghana*, report prepared for The British Council, Accra, Ghana.

Otter, S (1992) *Learning Outcomes in Higher Education*, London: Unit for the Development of Adult Continuing Education, Department of Employment.

Partington, P, Day, M, Jackson, N, O'Neil, M, Pennington, G and Wilson, A (1993) *Student Feedback: Context, issues and practice*, Sheffield: Committee of Vice-Chancellors and Principals/Universities' Staff Development Unit.

Pennington, G (1989) 'Staff development for enterprise in higher education: ten propositions', *Bulletin of Teaching and Learning*, 2, Newcastle: University of Northumbria.

Peters, R (1966) *Ethics and Education*, London: George Allen and Unwin.

Ramsden, P (ed.) (1988) *Improving Learning: New perspectives*, London: Kogan Page.

Ramsden, P (1992) *Learning to Teach in Higher Education*, London: Routledge.

Ramsden, P (1993) 'Theories of learning and teaching and the practice of excellence in higher education', *Higher Education Research and Development*, 12, 87–97.

Ramsden, P and Dodds, A (1989) *Improving Teaching and Courses*, Melbourne: Centre for the Study of Higher Education, University of Melbourne.

Reid, WA (1987) 'Institutions and practices: professional education reports and the language of reform', *Educational Researcher*, 16, 8, 10–15.

Revans, R (1982) *The Origins and Growth of Action Learning*, Bromley: Chartwell Bratt.

Revans, R (1991a) 'The concept, origin and growth of action learning', in Zuber-Skerritt, O (ed.) *Action Learning for Improved Performance*, Brisbane: AEBIS Publishing, pp.14–25.

Revans, R (1991b) 'Reg Revans Speaks About Action Learning', a video programme in the series 'Action Learning and Action Research' produced by O Zuber-Skerritt, TV Unit, The University of Queensland, Brisbane.

Richards, T and Richards, L (1991) *Data base organisation for qualitative analysis: The NUDIST System*, technical report no. 18/91, La Trobe University, Melbourne.

Robbins, Lord (1963) *Higher Education: Report of the committee*, (cmnd 2154), London: HMSO.

Roe, E and McDonald, R (1983) *Improved Professional Judgment*, St Lucia, Qld: University of Queensland Press.

Roe, E, McDonald, R and Moses, I (1986) *Reviewing Academic Performance*, St Lucia, Qld: University of Queensland Press.

Rogers, C (1983) *Freedom to Learn for the 80s*, London: Merrill.

Ryan, Y and Zuber-Skerritt, O (eds) (1994) *Departmental Excellence in University Education – Action research case studies*, Brisbane: Tertiary Education Institute, University of Queensland, no 4 in Occasional Papers Series.

Säljö, R (1988) 'Learning in educational settings: methods of inquiry', in Ramsden, P (ed.) *Improving Learning: New perspectives*, London: Kogan Page.

Samuelowicz, K and Bain, J (1992) 'Conceptions of teaching held by academic teachers', *Higher Education*, 24, 93–111.

Schön, D (1971) *Beyond the Stable State: Public and private learning in a changing society*, London: Temple Smith.

Schön, D (1983) *The Reflective Practitioner: How professionals think in action*, London: Temple Smith.

Schön, D (1987) *Educating the Reflective Practitioner*, San Francisco, CA: Jossey-Bass.

Senge, P (1990) *The Fifth Discipline: The art and practice of the learning organization*, New York: Doubleday.

Sieber, S (1972) 'Images of the practitioner and strategies of educational change', *Sociology of Education*, 45.

Smith, SL (1991) 'Quality control and performance indicators', a report of the Canadian Commission of Inquiry on Canadian University Education, Ottawa: Queen's Printer for Canada.

Stenhouse, L (1983) 'Research as a basis for teaching', in *Authority, Education and Emancipation*, London: Heinemann.

Stephenson, J and Weil, S (eds) (1992) *Quality in Learning: A capability approach in higher education*, London: Kogan Page.

Stephenson, J and Laycock, M (eds) (1993) *Using Learning Contracts in Higher Education*, London: Kogan Page.

Storey, S (1993) 'Total quality management through BS5750: a case study', in Ellis, R (ed.) *Quality Assurance for University Teaching*, Buckingham: SRHE and Open University Press.

Tate, A (1993) 'Quality in teaching and the encouragement of enterprise', in Ellis, R (ed.) *Quality Assurance for University Teaching*, Buckingham: SRHE and Open University Press, pp. 285–300.

Taylor, PG (1993) 'Focusing tertiary teaching on learning', paper delivered at the 5th European Conference of EARLI, Aix en Provence, 31 August to 5 September 1993.

Tight, M (1991) *Higher Education: A part-time perspective*, Milton Keynes: Society for Research into Higher Education and Open University Press.

Torbert, WR (1992) 'The true challenge of generating continual quality improvement', *Journal of Management Enquiry*, 4.

Trow, M (1992) 'Thoughts on the White Paper of 1991', *Higher Education Quarterly*, 46, 1, 213–26.

Warnock, M (1990) *Teaching Quality: Report of the committee of enquiry*, London: Polytechnics and Colleges Funding Council.

Warren Piper, D (1993) *Quality Management in Universities*, Canberra: Australian Government Publishing Service.

Watkins, P (1993) 'Centralised decentralisation: Sloanism, marketing quality and higher education', *Australian Universities' Review*, 36, 2, 9–15.

Weil, S (1992) 'Creating the capability for change in higher education: the RSA initiative', in Barnett, R (ed.) *Learning to Effect*, Buckingham: Society for Research into Higher Education and Open University Press.

Wright, P (1992) 'Learning through enterprise: the Enterprise in Higher Education Initiative', in Barnett, R (ed.) *Learning to Effect*, Buckingham: Society for Research into Higher Education and Open University Press.

Young, R (1989) *A Critical Theory of Education*, Hemel Hempstead: Harvester Wheatsheaf.

Zuber-Skerritt, O (1990) *Action Research for Change and Development*, Nathan Qld: Griffith University, Centre for the Advancement of Learning and Teaching.

Zuber-Skerritt, O (ed.) (1991) *Action Research for Change and Development*, Aldershot: Gower Avebury.

Zuber-Skerritt, O (1992a) *Professional Development in Higher Education: A theoretical framework for Action Research*, London: Kogan Page.

Zuber-Skerritt, O (1992b) *Action Research in Higher Education: Examples and reflections*, London: Kogan Page.

INDEX